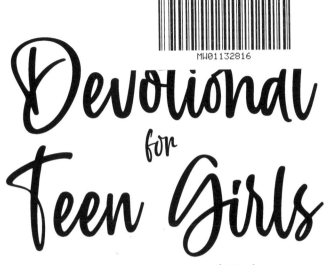

Devotional for Teen Girls

3-minute Devotions and Daily
Inspirations from the Bible for teenage
girls. Gratitude Journal for teens.

EILEEN NYBERG

ADISAN Publishing AB

Contents

Introduction

Being a teenager is difficult. You go through so much and learn so much about yourself and about life. You know who you can and can't trust. You also go through many changes with your body and body image. You deal with self-esteem issues and loss of friendships, death of family members or friends, or even your pets. You also deal with competition between you and other girls your age. You compete to see which of you is considered the most beautiful. You are thrust into the world of competition in sports and other competitions among friends. You also deal with bullying and people hurting your feelings. Then there is the issue of social media bullying and further stress that social media brings.

You may suffer from depression during your teenage years, too. However, there is hope in the name of Jesus. He has come to restore you from all of the stress that you're dealing with. He wants you to cast all your anxiety on Him. He doesn't want you to worry about what may happen tomorrow. He wants you to be at peace and to enjoy life to the fullest. Go to Him with any questions that you may have about life. He will guide you as you navigate through life.

We hope that this book offers you much hope and uplifts your spirits with whatever emotion you may be going through as a teenager. Know that you are never alone and you are never far from God's helping hand.

DEVOTION 1

I Am God's Child

*"...The Lord does not look at the things people
look at. People look at the outward appearance,
but the Lord looks at the heart."*
1 Samuel 16:7

How can I be aware and proud of who I am in Christ?

Have you ever been bullied because of your appearance at school? Have you ever thought negatively about yourself? Did you start thinking that you need makeup to be beautiful? If you've ever thought you needed to change your appearance to have kids stop making fun of you, try to remember who you are in Christ. You never have to be ashamed of your appearance. No matter what anyone at school thinks of you, God sees you as His beautiful daughter.

He loves you as you are. It truly does not matter what you look like, the abilities you have, or who makes fun of you; God sees your inner beauty. You're His beloved child. You are perfect in His sight. As this verse says, people look at outward appearances, but the Lord looks at the heart. The Lord knows the goodness of your heart, and He will protect you from bullying. God also sees other kids' hearts when they bully you. Instead of being annoyed at them for hurting you, you can pray for them to see the light and realize that bullying is wrong.

• •

Whenever you struggle with your appearance, say this prayer:
"Lord, thank you for reminding me that I never have to change
my appearance. Thank you, Lord, for seeing me as your part,
as your child."

8

DEVOTION 2

God Has a Plan for Me

"For I know the plans I have for you," declares the Lord,
"plans to prosper you and not to harm you, plans to give
you hope and a future."
Jeremiah 29: 11

Am I uncertain about what the future holds for me?

As a teenager, you get a lot of things thrown at you in life. There are questions about where you might be going to high school or what you might like to be when you grow up. Others may ask you how you are doing in school or on a sports team. You might even question who you can trust at school. You can easily get affected by all the choices you have to make in your life, and you might think that your plans won't work out.

The good news is that God has excellent plans for your life. He plans to give you a prosperous life, and He wants to give you hope and a great future. Trust that God will guide you in every area of your life, whether it's making friends, playing sports, or choosing what high school to go to. Be comforted that God already knows what will happen in your life. He has your future already lined up perfectly. Rest in His promises and His assurance to give you a great life.

• •

Whenever you're uncertain, say this prayer: "Lord, please help me to rest in your promises. Thank you that even if my plans don't work out, your plans will succeed. Thank you for giving me a great future."

DEVOTION 3

I Can Ask for His Help

*"For we are God's handiwork, created in
Christ Jesus to do good works, which God
prepared in advance for us to do."*
Ephesians 2:10

What do I struggle with as a teenager?

Have you ever thought you don't measure up to other kids' standards
in school or on the sports team? Are you struggling with schoolwork or
with fitting in on the sports team? Even though there are times where
you may feel inadequate, you can take comfort in the promise of this
scripture. You are God's masterpiece, created in Jesus' image to do
good works which God Himself has prepared for you to do. God will
help you excel in every area of your life? He'll help you figure out the
gifts He's given you. He'll help you use them to the best of your ability.

Even when you think that you don't measure up in certain areas of
your life, you will do amazing things in your life with God's help. Don't
beat yourself up just because things are taking longer for you. Don't be
afraid to ask God or others around you for help in any area of your life.
There is no discredit in asking for help when you need it.

Whatever you struggle with, you can tell God by saying this
prayer: "Lord, please guide me in life. Thank you that I'm
unique and special in your eyes. Help me to remember that I
can always ask for help whenever I need it."

DEVOTION 4

I Am Beautiful

"I praise you, because I am fearfully and wonderfully made; your works are wonderful, I know that full well."
Psalm 139:14

Do I appreciate both my inner and outer beauty?

What comes to mind when you think of beauty? A celebrity such as Margot Robbie? Do you think of someone you know, such as a friend or even someone you have a crush on at school? Everyday life has a lot of pressure on you as a young woman to look beautiful.

If you've ever thought that you're not beautiful enough because of the world's standards of beauty, you are beautiful in your family's eyes and in God's eyes. You're perfect just the way you are! You are fearfully and wonderfully made by God Himself. You are created for a beautiful and unique purpose. Even though school, embracing your body image and life can be difficult, you can learn to appreciate your inner and outer beauty. Remember, God's work in your life is lovely. Take time to figure out what your purpose is in life. Ask God for help in realizing your goal and then go after it with everything you have. Ask God for help with seeing your inner beauty. Cherish your uniqueness and embrace it.

• •

Whenever you struggle with your beauty, say this prayer: "Lord, please help me to embrace my unique looks and my unique abilities. Thank you for making me feel unique in your eyes and in my family's eyes. My beloved, please guide me to see myself through your eyes."

DEVOTION 5

Honor My Body

"......Do you not know that your bodies are temples of
the Holy Spirit, who is in you, whom you have received
from God? You are not your own; you were bought at a
price. Therefore, honor God with your bodies."
1 Corinthians 6:19-20

How can I resist the temptation to dishonor my body even
when it looks fun or is seen as the "in" thing to do?

Peer pressure is no joke, especially as a teenager. You may be pressured
to skip school, cheat on tests, or cheat on your sports team to help them
win. You may try to fit with the popular kids at school by doing other
harmful things to your body, such as smoking cigarettes or marijuana.

It's important to remember: you are not your own. When you want to
do things that harm your body, you're not honoring God or protecting
yourself. Your body is a holy temple, on rent to you from God. Your
body is a Church of the Holy Spirit. You can resist the temptation of
dishonoring your body by asking God to remind you that those sub-
stances do harm to your body. Honor your body by protecting it from
drugs, drinking, or smoking.

· ·

Whenever you face choices that might harm your body, you
can say this prayer: "Lord, please help me to protect my body
and honor it at all costs. Even if it means not fitting in with the
"the in-crowd."

DEVOTION 6

Learning Opportunity

*"But he said to me, "My grace is sufficient for you,
for my power is made perfect in weakness." "Therefore, I
will boast all the more gladly about my weaknesses, so
that Christ's power may rest on me. That is why,
for Christ's sake, I delight in weaknesses, in insults,
in hardships, in persecutions, in difficulties.
For when I am weak, then I am strong."*
2 Corinthians 12:9-10

How can I look at hard times as learning opportunities?

If you've ever been made fun of because of your appearance in school, or because you don't do things such as sports, acting, or something that other kids do, you aren't alone. Every time someone makes fun of you, it hurts, doesn't it? You might be thinking, why did God make me like this? Why am I weak?

Take comfort in this scripture. Even though you may not be at the same place as everyone else is in school, even when you think you're weak, you are strong because you have God on your side. You can boast about your weakness because God's power is made perfect in your weakness. Don't beat yourself up when someone insults you, ridicules you, mocks you, or when you go through a hard time. Instead, rejoice in all of those instances because they can actually teach you a lot and make you a healthier individual.

• •

Whenever someone hurts you, pray this prayer:
"Lord, please remind me I am strong, even if someone
insults me. Help me to learn to rejoice in my difficulties."

13

Never Doubt Myself

"........Trust in the Lord with all your heart and lean not on
your own understanding; in all your ways submit
to him, and he will make your paths straight."
Proverbs 3:5-6

Do I ever doubt myself and my abilities compared
to someone else's abilities?

Have you ever felt as though no matter how hard you try, things may never go correctly in your life? As a teenager, you're pulled in so many different directions. When things aren't going the way you'd like them to, in school, in your home life, in your friendships or relationships, you can ask yourself whether you are leaning on your own understanding or trusting God to get you through hard times in life. This scripture tells you not to rely on your own account.

Trust Him with all your heart. You might say to yourself, "How can I trust someone I can't see?" Think of it this way: When you relax on a plane, you can't see the pilot, but you hear him over the speaker telling you when you will be taking off and when you will be landing. The same thing is true with God. Even though you can't see Him, He is there guiding you. He will help you see His favor. Ask Him to help you see your blessings amongst your difficulties.

• •

Whenever you doubt yourself, you can pray this prayer
in your heart or out loud: "Lord, please help me to trust
you with every part of my life. I know you will
make my paths straight."

Gain in Confidence

"......I can do all things through
Christ who strengthens me."
Philippians 4:13

What tasks do I struggle with? How can I gain
the confidence that God is willing to give me?

Have you ever thought that you would never be able to do well in math class? How about feeling like you don't measure up on a sports team compared to someone else who has a lot of talent? Have you ever told yourself that you wouldn't be able to do specific tasks around the house or at your place of work? The pressure to succeed as a teenager can be overwhelming. Sometimes it seems as though there is no end in sight. You are always told how you must do things and conform to other people's ways of doing them. It can get very frustrating, and you may feel like giving up at times.

There is hope though. Just because you may not do things the way someone might like you to do them, it doesn't mean you're doing them in the wrong way. You could even show others new ways of getting math homework done or show your brother new ways to do chores. This scripture reminds you that you can do all things through Christ who gives you strength!

• •

When you feel pressure on all sides, pray this prayer: "Lord,
please remind me that, through you, I can and will accomplish
every task that you have put in front of me."

Endure Temptations

*"No temptation has overtaken you except what
is common to mankind. And God is faithful;
he will not let you be tempted beyond what you can
bear. But when you are tempted, he will also
provide a way out so that you can endure it."*
1 Corinthians 10:13

How can I resist temptations?

Have you encountered yourself being scared of what one of your friends was telling you to do? Have you ever been tempted to drink while you're underage or have premarital sex? How about trying different drugs? Have you ever experienced that feeling of the "good angel versus the bad angel" on your shoulder when being tempted? The good angel is the Holy Spirit telling you to walk away, while the evil angel is Satan messing with your head. Satan is very good at making you think that the temptation of drinking, doing drugs, or having premarital sex is no big deal. Any temptation can seem like it's no big deal until you see the consequences on the other side of that decision.

Every temptation you encounter has the potential to destroy your life. You have to make wise choices in every situation. The good news is that God won't let you be tempted beyond what you can bear. He will also give you a way out of every temptation.

Whenever you're tempted, you can say this prayer: "Lord, thank you for giving me a way out of every temptation. Thank you for giving me the strength to endure."

16

DEVOTION 10

Purpose in Life

*"And we know that for those who love God
all things work together for good, for those
who are called according to his purpose."*
Romans 8:28

Do I believe that I'm called according to His purpose?

No matter what you go through in your life, whether through trials in your personal life, in school, in your friendships, or in your relationships, take comfort knowing that God will make everything work together for your good and for His glory. Even though you may think that things can—and will—only get worse, God wants only what's best for you. Don't compare yourself to others or lower your expectations to fit in with people. You also don't have to stop doing the things God has put on your heart. Embrace your uniqueness. There is no one else like you! You are perfect the way you are.

You are called according to His purpose. Take the time to figure out what your God-given purpose is and then go after it with all of your heart. Seek the Divine intervention to help you find your purpose, and believe that you can—and will—make a difference for His kingdom.

• •

The next time you doubt your purpose, say this prayer: "Lord,
please help me to remember that I'm called according to your
purpose and not my own. Thank you
for giving me your divine purpose in my life.
Help me to live it well."

DEVOTION 11

Hope during Struggles

"Not only so, but we also glory in our
sufferings, because we know that suffering produces
perseverance; perseverance, character; and character,
hope. And hope does not put us to shame, because God's
love has been poured out into our hearts through the
Holy Spirit, who has been given to us."
Romans 3:3-5

How can I rejoice and be glad even amid my sufferings?

What is the hardest struggle that you've gone through in your life so far? Have you lost a loved one, or maybe a relationship or a friendship? Everyone has gone through those things at one time or another. You can cry, be mad, be upset, and question God, asking Him why those things happened the way they did; he wants you to come to Him with anything and everything that's on your mind.

You can accept in front of God that you struggle. He also wants to remind you that you can still rejoice in your sufferings because they result in a fighting spirit, which produces character, and character makes hope. You're allowed to have hope even during your struggles. You don't have to be ashamed to tell anyone that you have the hope of Christ within you, either.

The next time you find yourself struggling, say this prayer:
"Lord, please remind me that I can rejoice in my sufferings
and that I don't have to be ashamed to have hope during
my struggles. Thank you that your love is with me
every step of the way."

Grief after Loss

"Where, O death, is your victory?
Where, O death, is your sting?"
1 Corinthians 15:55

Do I believe Jesus' promise of eternal life?

Losing a beloved is a pain like no other. It's raw and cuts you deep within your heart. Often your question how you will ever get past the grief and the anguish of losing that person. You may even go through periods of depression, despair, and even denial that the person is really gone.

All of those emotions are common, and it's completely okay to feel grief in different stages. The grieving process is different and unique, as is the mechanism of coping with loss. The great news is that anyone who believes in Jesus Christ as their Lord and Savior will never die. If your loved one believes in Jesus as their Savior, then they have eternal life in Heaven! They are waiting for you in Heaven, and you can have comfort knowing that you will see them again when you get there.

· ·

Whenever you go through grief, remember this prayer:
"Lord, I thank you that your promises are true. Thank you that I will see my loved one in Heaven again one day! Thank you that, through my salvation in Jesus, death doesn't ever get to have the final victory."

Strength and Energy

*"....When a woman has a discharge of blood for
many days at a time other than her monthly period
or has a discharge that continues beyond her period, she
will be unclean as long as she has the discharge, just as
in the days of her period."*
Leviticus 15:25

How do I combat the symptoms of my period?

As a young woman, you will go through many changes. You will hit puberty, and you will experience your first period. You will bleed for up to seven days. There will probably be cramping and pain in your stomach, and you might have to take over-the-counter medications to combat the cramps. This is a regular occurrence for every woman, ages 13 and older. It will generally occur every month. You could be in school, at work, or at home when you experience bleeding for the first time. It will cause your emotions—and your hormones—to be out of whack.

However, you don't have to worry about your period because, even in your embarrassment and pain, God is walking with you through it. He will give you the power and the strength to forge through your daily tasks, even when you're on your period. Pray for less pain and for the energy to get through your period every month, and God will grant your requests.

. . . .

When you start your period, remember this prayer:
"Lord, I believe that you will give me energy and strength to
get through my periods every month. Thank you for making
them less painful."

Guidance to Handle Pain

"....When she is cleansed from her discharge,
she must count off seven days, and after that
she will be ceremonially clean."
Leviticus 15:28

Do I feel much better emotionally and physically
after my period is over every month?

Generally, on the eighth day after your period started, it will end. This, of course, is different for every girl's body. Some periods can last eight or more days. Some girls have a longer time between each of their periods, depending on how much they weigh and their stress level. If it lasts too long, you may need to make an appointment with your doctor to see what could be going on.

The good news is that when your period stops, you are considered clean again for the next month. It is essential to keep track of when your period started and when it ended, so you know how many days are in between each of your periods. Don't you feel much more relieved, and a lot calmer, and even a lot cleaner when you get to the end of your period? God is the one who causes periods to begin and end. He will be with you every time yours happens. Trust that He will relieve your pain and make you clean again.

• •

Every time you get your period, you can say this prayer: "Lord, please be with me in the midst of my period. Help my pain to be low, and help the bleeding to be minimal. Thank you for making me clean from it every month."

DEVOTION 15

Sexual Temptations

"........It is God's will that you should be sanctified: that you should avoid sexual immorality; that each of you should learn to control your own body in a way that is holy and honorable, not in passionate lust like the pagans, who do not know God..."
1 Thessalonians 4:3-5

Have I ever had sex or thought about having
sex with someone before marriage?

You shouldn't give in to sexual temptations, no matter what. Even if you feel as if it'll be no big deal or think, "Oh come on, I love this person. It's just this once." Even if it only happens once, sex before marriage is a sin. You should learn to control your body from a young age to not fall into sexual temptation.

Later in your life, no matter who you're dating, you need to wait to have sex with the person you're going to marry. Then once you get married, your sex life will be much more intimate, sacred, and blessed by God. You have to do your best to resist sexual temptation to keep your body holy in the eyes of God.

• •

The next time you're tempted to have sex outside of marriage, you can say this prayer in your heart or out loud: "Lord, please help me to remember that sex before marriage is a sin in your eyes. Help me to not lust after anyone that I'm in a relationship with. Help me to be able to control myself and my body."

Sex before Marriage

"....If anyone is worried that he might not be acting honorably toward the virgin he is engaged to, and if his passions are too strong and he feels he ought to marry, he should do as he wants. He is not sinning. They should get married...."
1 Corinthians 7:36-38

Has my boyfriend approached me and wanted to have sex with me outside of marriage? How can I help remind him that we shouldn't have sex outside of marriage?

Just because a man is engaged to you, and has strong, loving feelings towards you, doesn't mean that premarital sex isn't a sin. If your boyfriend's passion towards you is too strong and he wants to have sex with you because he loves you, explain to him that you both should wait until after you're married to engage in sex.

If your union together is ordained by God, and you know deep in your heart you should get married and ask God to continue to bless the relationship. God will bless it even more if you wait until after you're married before having sex.

• •

The next time you think about having sex before you're married, pray this prayer in your heart: "Lord, please lead me to be with the right man when my time comes to be married. Help us want to save sex until after marriage because we know it is the right thing. Please bless our union and help us to remain sexually pure until we are married."

23

DEVOTION 17

Monogamous Relationship

".....But since sexual immorality is occurring,
each man should have sexual relations with his own wife,
and each woman with her own husband...."
1 Corinthians 7:2

When I get married, I should only have sex
with my husband and no one else.

Everyone will experience sexual immorality at one time or another. As a teen, your body changes, and you hit puberty. You will be tempted to have sex with your boyfriend before he becomes your husband. The person you're with now as a teenager may not become your husband later in your life. It is vital to save yourself until marriage with the right person that God ordains you to be with.

When you get married, you should only have sex with the person you are married to. Having multiple partners for sex without connection can lead to adultery, also known as cheating. Likewise, your husband shouldn't cheat on you or ever have sex with anyone other than you. Love and sex are considered a sacred act between a man and a woman.

• •

If you find yourself thinking about premarital sex, say this prayer: "Lord, please help me and my future husband to not engage in sex with anyone else before we are married. Bless our union together and help us to stay sexually pure. Keep temptation away from both of us and help us remember to stay committed to each other all our days."

DEVOTION 18

Turn Your Stress to God

"Trouble and distress have come upon me,
but your commands give me delight."
Psalm 119:143

What am I stressing about in my life?
How can I give the stress over to God?

Stress can come upon you when you least expect it, whether it's stress with friends, your family, even within your own body. You can have fallings out with friends that you thought would be in your life forever. It can be challenging to overcome rifts in friendships sometimes, even though both sides may try their hardest.

You can also have arguments with your parents about responsibilities such as chores, curfews, and even fights over your parent's advice may give you about approaching different areas of your life. These areas include friendships, schoolwork, and relationships. It might be hard to open up to your parents and explain how you feel about their rules.

You can also have stress when you hit puberty and your period starts. Your emotions and hormones will be out of whack, and it can all be hard to understand. You may be uncomfortable or in pain at those times. Even in those stressors as a teen, God wants you to take comfort in His words. His commands can give you delight. As long as you walk in His ways, you will be able to face any struggles head-on.

• •

Whenever you're stressed out, you can say this prayer: "Lord,
thank you that I can turn to you, even though
stress and trouble will come in my life."

Worrying about Tests

"...Therefore, do not worry about tomorrow,
for tomorrow will worry about itself.
Each day has enough trouble of its own."
Mathew 6:34

How do I keep from worrying about tomorrow?

School tests can cause a lot of stress in your life. If you struggle with particular subjects, whether it's math, reading, English, or science, sometimes it feels even though you try hard and learn the material, you just don't understand it. You feel the pressure mount on you to get good grades to get into an excellent high school and then into a good college. You can stay up, studying into the night, wondering if you know the material well enough. Worrying about a test that is coming up can cause you to have irritability, insomnia, headaches, and even digestive issues. Stress can wreak havoc on your body.

You don't have to worry about any tests that are coming up in school. Whether the test is tomorrow, the next day, or next week, you should only be focused on the day that's in front of you. God tells you that you don't have to worry about tomorrow because it will have its own problems. You must trust in Him and believe that everything will work out. Trust that He will help you through any test in school and in life.

Whenever you find yourself worrying about a test, try saying
this prayer: "Lord, thank you for the reminder
to not worry about tomorrow. Help me to just
stay focused on today."

DEVOTION 20

Fight with A Friend

"......*The Lord will fight for you;*
you need only to be still."
Exodus 14:14

How can I be still in God's presence?

When you have a falling out with a friend, whether it's a competition over a boy's affections or an argument that started on social media or texting, it can be hard to go through. Remember the last time you had a fight with your friend. How did you react to it? Were you in shock over what happened or in denial?

You may have tried to talk to your other friend(s) or family members about the disagreement, but they may not have been able to help you because they didn't want to take sides. You may have tried talking to your friend, trying to apologize to them, and work the situation out. You may have tried to be the bigger person. If they didn't want to talk things through, at least you know that you tried your hardest. Be still and let God fight that battle for you. He might even help you mend the friendship in a different way.

• •

The next time you go through a friendship battle, try saying this prayer: "Lord, please help me to remember that I can be still and turn over any and all of my battles to you. Thank you for fighting for me."

DEVOTION 21

Calm My Anxieties

"Do not be anxious about anything, but in every situation,
by prayer and petition, with thanksgiving, present your
requests to God......"
Philippians 4:6

What is causing me anxiety? How can I overcome it?

What causes you anxiety? Maybe it's schoolwork, homework, sports, being alone, or being in a room full of people. Perhaps you get pressure from taking tests in school or giving oral reports/debates in grade school or high school. Have you ever felt anxiety from your home life? Maybe you worry about your family's finances or the future. Stress can wreak havoc on your mind, body, and soul if you allow it to.

Even though it seems that there are a million and one things to be anxious about, God reassures you that you don't have to be worried about anything. Instead, you can present your anxieties, requests, and fears in front of God with thanksgiving in your heart. You might be asking, "How can I have thanksgiving in my heart amid the anxieties that I'm struggling with?" Bring your anxiety to God without the fear of judgment or condemnation. He wants to help you through any and all of your worries. Call on Him and ask Him to calm your mind, body, and spirit.

• •

The next time you feel anxious, say this prayer: "Lord, thank you that I can come to you with any and all of my anxieties without fear of judgment or condemnation. Help me to give thanks despite my circumstances."

Whenever You Get Tired

*"...Come to me, all you who are weary and burdened, and
I will give you rest."*
Mathew 11:28

What am I weary from?

Too many activities can make you exhausted—everything from sports practice to completing schoolwork, studying for tests, and completing homework. You can also get weary from trying to measure up to people's standards in life, whether it's the expectations your parents put on you, the expectations that you put on yourself, or the teacher's expectations of you. As a teenager, the pressures of life can be enormous. It can seem as though you're running a million miles an hour with no end in sight. Life, in general, can wear you down.

Jesus would want you to come to Him if you are feeling weary, and He will give you rest. He wants you to feel refreshed and recharged every day, not lethargic and weighed down by the constant busyness of life. You can turn to Him any time, day or night, and get a much-needed refresher for your body, soul, and mind. Read your Bible every day, or read a devotional. Pray for peace and strength to make it through another day. He will give you the power that you didn't know you needed.

Whenever you're weary, try saying this prayer:
"Lord, please help me to turn to you whenever
I feel weary from the stress and pace of life."

Warm up to Goodness

"...For physical training is of some value, but godliness has value for all things, holding promise for both the present life and the life to come....."
1 Timothy 4:8

How do I train my mind, body, and soul to become Godly each and every day?

You do a lot of training if you work out or are on a soccer, lacrosse, basketball, or baseball team. What do you do to get your body ready before practicing or before a game? You stretch your muscles, so you don't get cramps. When you work out, you start out slowly and work your way up to heavier weights, so you don't strain your muscles. Even when you run, you start by running slowly to warm up your lungs. You don't just sprint across the basketball court or the field without warming up.

In the same way, you can also warm up your mind, body, and soul to the goodness of God in your life by reading His word every day, helping those who are in need, and being a light in this broken world. Remember, physical training is essential, but Godliness has value above all other things. Being Godly holds promise for you in your present life and your future life as a citizen of Heaven. It may be essential to work out your body, but working out your soul is even more critical.

. . . .

Before warming up for a game, you can pray this prayer:
"Lord, thank you for showing me what's really
important in life."

DEVOTION 24

Beauty Competition

"Charm is deceptive, and beauty is fleeting;
but a woman who fears the Lord is to be praised."
Proverbs 31:30

Am I worried about how people see me,
or am I more concerned about knowing God?

Beauty competition is in magazines, on TV, and on social media. There will always be someone that you think looks more beautiful than you. You can wear yourself thin, comparing your looks to other girls at school. You may think, "She's more beautiful than me. She has more friends than I do. Why is she getting all the boys' phone numbers, and not one guy is looking at me, even as a friend, much less as a girlfriend? What do I have to do to get noticed by people at school?"

You may go to great lengths to make yourself look more beautiful according to the world's standards. You may buy different makeup brands and try new styles of clothing and unique hairstyles to impress people in your class. All of that is common as a teenager, but the critical thing to remember is that charm and beauty are fleeting. If you are a woman who loves the Lord, you are doing the right thing in your life. Think about how you can be a reflection of Him to your classmates instead of thinking you aren't beautiful.

• •

Whenever you struggle with beauty, say this prayer:
"Lord, please remind me that following you is the
divine thing I can ever do in life."

Dressing Provocatively

*"I also want the women to dress modestly,
with decency and propriety, adorning themselves,
not with elaborate hairstyles or gold or pearls or
expensive clothes, but with good deeds, appropriate
for women who profess to worship God."*
1 Timothy 2:9-10

Am I dressing in a way that's pleasing to God?

Have you ever seen other girls dressing provocatively? Maybe they are trying to impress the boys at school by the way they dress. Have you ever wanted to dress like that, to be seen? As tempting as it may seem to dress immodestly, it is crucial to think of who you are dressing for. Are you seeking attention?

It's important to dress nicely and modestly, so you look like a mature young woman. You don't need to flaunt your hair or your body to any-one who will look. In fact, if you do that often, people might think you're trying too hard. As it says in this Bible verse, you never need to put on fancy clothes or try the "in" hairdos styles to impress people or to get people to notice you. You also don't have to buy expensive jewelry to put on every time you go out. Instead, you should want to dress nicely and maturely so that you please and worship God. You can honor God by wearing modest clothing.

The next time you're tempted to dress provocatively, you can say this prayer: "Lord, please help me want to dress in a way that's pleasing to you."

Tattoos and Piercings

"Do not cut your bodies for the dead or put tattoo marks on yourselves. I am the Lord."
Leviticus 19:28

How can I honor God with my body?

As you get older, you might see many people at school or at work with tattoos all over their bodies. Have you looked at a tattoo and thought, "Wow, that looks so cool! It looks so awesome. I want to get one?" A tattoo, once done, is impossible to remove from your body?

Did you know that the people who give tattoos put needles with ink into your skin to give you the tattoos? If your pain threshold is not high, it is not a good idea to get one. You don't want to cause yourself needless pain just to get a tattoo. If the tattoo is messed up, it becomes almost impossible to fix. You do not need tattoos to fit in with the "in" crowd. Also, it is not pleasing to God for you to get a tattoo. In the Bible, it warns against you putting tattoos on your body. It also warns against cutting or making marks on your body for the dead. Rather than doing those things to fit in, remember that it is more important to please God by honoring your body.

· ·

The next time you're tempted to get a tattoo, you can say this prayer: "Lord, please help me to honor my body in a way that is pleasing to you."

Courage during Hard Times

*"She is clothed with strength and dignity;
she can laugh at the days to come."*
Proverbs 31: 25

Do I believe that I'm clothed with strength
and dignity from God?

There will be hard days ahead for you in your life. As a teenager, the pressures of succeeding in life are enormous. Even on the days when you think you can't go on with school or work, you can remember that you are a child of God. You are chosen for a great purpose and have a great destiny. Even during your hard times, you can rest in God's assurance and believe in His promises. You are clothed with strength and dignity in your life. Believe that His words are trustworthy and declare them over your life every day. Talk positively about your life instead of negatively.

Once you start declaring God's promises over your life, it will be much easier to believe in them. You will walk with God's power within you. You will have peace in your life, even amongst any chaos, turmoil, or trials that you encounter. You trust that God will get you through any and all of the hard times in your life. You can laugh at the future instead of dreading it, thanks to God.

• •

Whenever you have a hard day, you can say this prayer: "Lord, I thank you that I'm clothed with strength and dignity in my life. Fill me with your peace so I can laugh at the days that are ahead."

Inner Beauty

"You are altogether beautiful, my darling;
there is no flaw in you."
Song of Solomon 4:7

Do I struggle to believe that I'm beautiful
in God's eyes?

Have you ever come home from school crying because another girl got picked as the cheerleading squad captain or the basketball team captain? Have you ever been jealous that another girl was crowned homecoming queen when you thought you deserved it more? How about coming home from school in tears because one of your friends has a boyfriend now? Not being picked for individual teams or not having a boyfriend when other girls have one can hurt a lot when you're a teenager. But you are still beautiful in your own unique ways.

You are altogether beautiful, no matter how anyone sees you at school or on the sports team. Even if you don't have a boyfriend yet, God sees nothing wrong with you. Even if you weren't picked for the position you wanted in school or on the sports team, God still chooses you. He sees you as His beloved daughter. Your heavenly father finds no fault or flaw in you! Isn't that amazing? No one's opinion of you matters as much as God's opinion of you.

The next time you struggle with inner beauty, you can say this prayer: "Lord, thank you for reminding me that I am beautiful and chosen in your eyes. Thank you that you don't see any flaws or faults in me."

DEVOTION 29

Afraid of Circumstances

"So do not fear, for I am with you;
do not be dismayed, for I am your God.
I will strengthen you and help you; I will uphold you with
my righteous right hand."
Isaiah 41:10

How can I overcome my fears with God's help?

Whenever you go through difficult times, such as friendship trouble or a family member's illness, you can lose hope. Everything can look hopeless in either of those situations. You can pray for that friendship to be restored and for your family member to be healed. Even though you're praying, do you sometimes doubt God's goodness in your life? Every teenager goes through times of questioning God. You're not alone. Even though your fears and doubts, God invites you to come to Him with your prayer requests.

He wants you to not be dismayed or frightened by your circumstances because He is with you. Even when you feel as though you can't go on, He will fill you with His. He will strengthen you and uplift you with His righteous right hand. He will not let you continue to slip into despair. He doesn't want you to live in misery because of a family member being ill or because a friendship doesn't work out. He is always there to help you. All you have to do is ask Him.

• •

The next time you're afraid, say this prayer: "Lord, thank you for always being there for my family and me. Please help me to trust in you in all circumstances."

36

DEVOTION 30

Strengthen My Body

"Look to the Lord and his strength;
seek his face always."
1 Chronicles 16:11

Am I seeking His strength or relying on
my own strength?

Physical fitness is essential in your life. Working out makes you stronger. What do you do to work out your body? Do you lift weights, run, do yoga, or compete on different sports teams at school? Physical fitness not only helps you to become stronger, but it also helps you build endurance and handle things in life better. Being on a sports team makes you more disciplined and teaches you to work with others as a team.

It is important to continually seek God's goodness in everything you do. It is also essential to exercise your mind and faith daily by reading the Bible, reading devotionals, and engaging with other believers. Seek His strength, and you will discover the power inside you that you didn't know was there. Seek His goodness in every area of your life, and you will see the beauty in everything. You can seek Him by keeping Him close in every area of your life. You don't have to wear yourself thin physically every day either. You can seek God's strength every day.

The next time you feel yourself being worn thin, you can say this prayer: "Lord, please help me to continually seek you in all that I do. Please help me to not only strengthen my body physically but to strengthen my faith spiritually every day."

Keeping the Faith

"For no word from God will ever fail."
Luke 1:37

Have I ever doubted God? How do I keep the faith?

Like every other teenager, you have big questions about your life. You may wonder about who your friends will be in middle school or high school. You may wonder about what job you will take, or what college you're going to. You also wonder how God's plan will play out in your life. Sometimes it is tempting to take your life out of God's hands and try to make it in your own power. You might think that you can figure things out on your own without His help. However, that couldn't be further from the truth. When you try to take your life into your own hands, you will feel physically and emotionally exhausted. You will wonder what you have gotten yourself into.

The good news is that you can always come back to your senses—and back to God's presence—at any time, whether it's day or night. Ask for His forgiveness for thinking you could do things your own way instead of according to His way. He will forgive you and welcome you back with open arms. No word from Him in your life will ever fail. Trust that His ways are better than yours. He has a more fantastic plan for your life than you could ever imagine.

. . . .

Even if you walk away from God, you can return to Him by saying this prayer: "Lord, thank you that your plans never fail!"

DEVOTION 32

Attention Seeking

"Be careful not to practice your righteousness in front of others to be seen by them. If you do, you will have no reward from your Father in heaven."
Mathew 6:1

Am I posting on social media for recognition?

When you post your accomplishments on social media, what is your ultimate goal? To get people to like, comment, and be proud of you and commend you for the things you've accomplished? Do you ever feel unworthy when someone doesn't validate or comment on the things you posted? Don't be discouraged by the lack of Facebook likes, Instagram loves, or lack of comments on accomplishments posted on social media.

Just because you don't get recognition on social media doesn't mean you're being ignored. God still sees you. It even warns you in the Bible not to seek the praise of others. If you strive for too much reward on Earth, you won't have any rewards waiting for you when you get to Heaven. Do not be self-righteous about the things you do in your life. Instead, keep a humble attitude about the things you have accomplished and even the things you have yet to complete. There is nothing wrong with being proud of your accomplishments, but be careful not to brag and think too highly of yourself.

• •

The next time you seek attention, ask God to change your heart. Try saying this prayer instead: "Lord, thank you for reminding me to be humble about my accomplishments and to not seek the attention of others."

God is My Refuge

"The Lord is a refuge for the oppressed,
a stronghold in times of trouble."
Psalm 9:9

Am I seeking God as my refuge?

Have you ever thought all hope was lost? When you go through the hard times in junior high and high school, you can seek God for comfort because He is your ever-present help in times of trouble. Whether you're struggling to fit in, or with being comfortable reading out loud in class, or feeling like you don't measure up on the sports team, God can be your refuge among all of those hardships. He can also be your stronghold in times of trouble.

All you have to do is call upon Him, and He will hear your pleas and cries for help. He will guide you with the right words to say when you are called on in class. He will help you fit in on any sports team or any other group you're a member of. He will help you refine your skills on the sports team to make a good impression on your coaches. He will give you Godly friendships that will last a lifetime. He can and will help you get good grades in school, even in your most challenging subjects. You can rest assured that He will guide you through any struggles in school.

The next time you start to lose hope in school, you can say
this prayer: "Lord, thank you for delivering me from my strife
in school."

DEVOTION 34

Valley of Darkness

*"Even though I walk through the darkest valley,
I will fear no evil, for you are with me;
your rod and your staff, they comfort me."*
Psalm 23:4

What is the darkest valley that I've gone
through in life?

It can feel as though you're walking in a valley of darkness, confusion, fear, and uncertainty during your teenage years. You may not know how to ask people for help or how to even call on God to ask Him for help getting through it. Think for a few minutes: What is the darkest valley that you've gone through? Was it not fitting in with friends, struggles in school, the death of a pet, the death of a family member, or a falling out with a friend? Did you fear the future, and what lay ahead?

God wants you to remember that, even in the darkest and most confusing times of your life, you don't have to fear or give in to what Satan puts into your mind because God is with you. For example, he might make you think that you'll never succeed in life because you're struggling so hard in school or that you will never make any lasting friendships. On the contrary, God will help you in school, and He will bless you with true friendships that will last a lifetime.

. . . .

The next time you go through a dark valley,
say this prayer: "Lord, thank you that you're always with me,
even during the most difficult times of my life."

41

DEVOTION 35

Healing through Grieving

"...weeping may stay for the night,
but rejoicing comes in the morning."
Psalm 30:4

How can I rejoice when I lose someone I love?

Have you ever lost a family member? Losing someone you love is never easy. You can feel grief because they aren't on earth with you anymore. You can also feel guilt from the things that may not have been worked out between the two of you. You may even experience anger at God for taking them too soon. Feeling all of those emotions and working through them is entirely okay. However, God knew when their time to go home was going to happen. Your family member is now in Heaven with Jesus for all eternity.

If they struggle with an illness or addiction, let it bring you much comfort that they no longer have the illness, addiction, or disease. The bodies are made new, and they are whole. Sure, you will miss them for the rest of the time you're here on Earth, but you can rejoice to know that they are in paradise and that you will see them again when you get to Heaven. Your sorrow may last for the night, but God's joy comes in the morning.

To help remind yourself that you can rejoice even when you lose someone you love, you can say this prayer in your heart or out loud: "Lord, help me through this grieving process. Thank you that I will get to see my loved one again when I get to Heaven."

DEVOTION 36

Being Bullied

*"But those who hope in the Lord will renew their
strength. They will soar on wings like eagles;
they will run and not grow weary;
they will walk and not be faint."
Isaiah 40:31*

How do I keep my hope in the Lord instead of on Earthly things?

When you are being bullied in school, it can be hard to concentrate. Your grades may suffer, your self-esteem may take a hit. You may even feel depressed. If you've ever had thoughts about suicide because of bullying, please tell someone how you're feeling. Tell anyone that you can trust. Please get help from a trusted friend, s family member, a teacher, or a counselor. There is no shame in asking for help.

Remember, absolutely nothing is worth killing yourself over. If you're being bullied, tell someone about it. Make the school aware of it. Make your coach, teachers, and even the principal aware of what is happening to you. Most importantly, keep your faith in God because He is the main one who will see you through. He will help you figure out ways to get away from the bullies and how to stand up to them.

Just as this verse says, those who put their hope in the Lord will renew their strength. Do your best to seek God and ask Him for guidance in that situation.

• •

If you're being bullied, try saying this prayer: "Lord, please help me to remember that you're with me if I'm being bullied. Help me to be strong and to speak out."

Learning Difficulties

*"Jesus replied, "What is impossible
with man is possible with God."*
Luke 18:27

What subject seems impossible to me
in school right now?

What subjects do you struggle with in school? Do you struggle with math, science, social studies, or English? You're not alone. A lot of teens struggle in school. Have you ever felt like you'll never learn enough before a big test? You may doubt yourself and your abilities to retain the information, but you are smart! Even though you may think you'll never learn the material, you can learn the material with God's help.

Ask Him to help you understand the subject that you're struggling with. Don't be afraid to ask for help from one of your friends, a family member, or even ask your teacher for help. Think of ways you can learn the material faster. Make flashcards, read out loud, quiz yourself. You can even start a study group with your friends to go over the material before the big test. Quiz each other to see how much of the material you know. Working together, you can all learn the material faster. You can ask one of your friends who knows the material better to give you one-on-one tutoring as well. Remember, you can pass this test that you have coming up because nothing is impossible for God.

Whenever you're facing impossible odds in school, you can
remind yourself to say this prayer out loud or in your heart:
"Lord, thank you that nothing is impossible for you."

DEVOTION 38

Abuse in a Relationship

"The righteous cry out, and the Lord hears them;
he delivers them from all their troubles.
The Lord is close to the brokenhearted and
saves those who are crushed in spirit."
Psalm 34:17-18

Am I in an abusive relationship?

When you're in a new relationship with someone, all you'll feel at first is electricity and sparks. As you get to know someone, though, the truth comes out. Sometimes the truth is beautiful, but other times it can be gruesome. If you think you may be in an abusive relationship but aren't sure, here are some things to be on the lookout for. He takes your phone from you. He insists you do everything with him and only him. He isolates you from your friends and family. He physically or emotionally hurts you in any way.

If you see any of these signs, you need to get out of that relationship as soon as possible. You might be wondering, "How can I leave if he is threatening me?" Make a plan of escape with your friends or family if you can, and execute the plan. If you need to, then, by all means, call the police. Ask God for guidance and a way out, and He will give you one. He will deliver you from the relationship and bring you to safety.

. . . .

If you recognize that you're in an abusive relationship, start
saying this prayer: "Lord, please let me recognize the red flags
in this relationship and get out safely."

DEVOTION 39

Feeling Lonely

"The Lord himself goes before you and will be
with you; he will never leave you nor forsake you.
Do not be afraid; do not be discouraged."
Deuteronomy 31:8

Do I believe that God will never leave me?

Have you ever thought that you are unlovable? Has your family abandoned you? Have you ever thought you would never find true friends or have a boyfriend? Everyone feels unloved by their family at some time. Feeling unloved as a teen is no different. When you feel unloved by your family or that your family isn't giving you the kind of love you deserve, try talking to them about it calmly and see how they respond to your comments. If they say that they're sorry and want to make a better effort with you, then allow them the chance to do that.

If they don't accept the way you feel, you can start looking for other people to call your family. Look at the people in your school, your church group, and your Bible study and see who you can contact your family in those groups. The most important thing to remember is that, even if you're feeling alone or like you have no one to turn to, God will never leave you or forsake you. Even if you feel lonely, God is still with you.

The next time you feel lonely or abandoned, say this prayer:
"Lord, thank you that you will never abandon me. Thank you
that you're always with me."

DEVOTION 40

Introducing God to a Friend

"Jesus said to her, "I am the resurrection and the life. The one who believes in me will live, even though they die; and whoever lives by believing in me will never die. Do you believe this?"
John 11:25-26

Am I nervous to tell my friends about God?

Do you have a friend that doesn't know Jesus? Are you afraid to talk to them about Him or fearful of what their reaction will be? If you're unsure of what to say to them, pray about talking to them about Jesus. Ask Him for the right words and the right timing to bring up Jesus and how much He means in your life. When the right time comes, say a prayer, then take a step out in faith. Just be yourself and say what is on your heart about Him. You can tell them how Jesus has changed your life for the better and how He can help change their life too.

You can bring up your favorite Bible verses and your favorite Christian songs. You can share some of your favorite songs with your friend on the spot. If they are interested in learning more about Jesus, you can mention the verse above about Mary and Martha's brother Lazarus being raised from the dead from John 11:20-26. Offer to pray with them. Ask them to receive Jesus as their Lord and Savior.

Whenever you want to share Jesus' love with a friend,
say this prayer: "Lord, please help my friend to receive
you as their Savior."

DEVOTION 41

Comfort a Grieving Friend

*"Blessed are those who mourn,
for they will be comforted."*
Mathew 5:4

How can I comfort a friend who has
just lost a loved one?

Watching a friend mourn over their loved one's death can be one of the hardest things to do. You may not know what to do or say. You may be unsure how you can comfort them in the way they need to be settled. Ask God for guidance. You can write them a sympathy card, bring them flowers, or make them a warm meal, so they don't have to cook for themselves. You can even ask them if they'd like to go on a walk with you, or if they'd like to get coffee with you if they feel up to going out.

The most important thing you can do is pray for them and be there for them in their hour of mourning. The Bible says, "Blessed are those who mourn for they will be comforted." Even if you don't know what to say to them, sometimes just the fact that you're with them during their grief can be a great comfort to them. You don't have to say anything, just listen to them when they talk and never interrupt them. If you let them pour out their heart, then they know they can be honest with you.

• •

Any time you want to comfort a friend who is grieving, you can
say this prayer: "Lord, thank you for allowing me to be there
for my friend who is mourning."

Helping a Friend to Keep Faith

*"For no one is cast off by the Lord forever.
Though he brings grief, he will show compassion,
so great is his unfailing love."*
Lamentations 3:31-32

How can I help a grieving friend know that
God is still with them?

Have you ever had a friend struggle to keep the faith when they just lost a loved one? Here are some things that you can do to help them remember that God is still with them. You can remind them that their loved one is no longer suffering and isn't in sorrow anymore. Remind them of the victory that their family member has in Jesus Christ. You can remind them to rejoice that their loved one is in Heaven and that they have the hope that they will see them again one day in eternity.

You can also share your favorite songs to cheer them up. Bring them their favorite coffee or their favorite snack. Distract them with funny memes, or social media posts, or funny videos to make them laugh. Watch their favorite series or favorite movie with them. Remind them that even though there is grief now, the Lord will show their family compassion and His unfailing love.

The next time you're trying to help a friend who is suffering, you can say this prayer out loud or in your heart: "Lord, please help me to remind my hurting friend of your love in their time of sadness and grief. Please give me the right words to say to them at the right time."

DEVOTION 43

Fascination about Technology

"I have the right to do anything," you say—but not everything is beneficial. "I have the right to do anything"—but I will not be mastered by anything."
1 Corinthians 6:12

Do I have an addiction to technology?

Are you wasting time on your computer or TV? As a teenager, you might think that you have the right to do anything you want to in life. You might think you're allowed to watch as much TV or spend as much time on the computer as you'd like. Cell phones aren't the only addiction for teenagers. There are videogames, TVs, and computers, especially if you have a TV or computer in your room.

As it says in the Bible, not everything you do daily is beneficial to you. Sitting in front of a computer or watching TV all day doesn't help stimulate your brain. It makes you lazy. Being on a computer opens up doors to chat rooms where predators can lurk behind every screen, even if you're extremely careful. Instant messaging can be unhealthy, too, because you don't get to hear other people's reactions. Technology makes you think you know people when the reality is you don't know who you're talking to. Ask God to get you away from technology so you can start enjoying other aspects of your life.

· ·

The next time you're dealing with technology, say this prayer:
"Lord, please help curb my technology addiction. Help me to
see what is and isn't beneficial to me in my daily life."

Losing a Friendship

*"You turned my wailing into dancing; you removed
my sackcloth and clothed me with joy."*
Psalm 30:11

How can I keep the joy in my heart during
difficult times with my friends?

Have you ever lost a friendship when you thought the person would be in your life forever? Did they give you some closure, or did they leave you wondering what went wrong? You might be upset and question God about why that friend was taken out of your life. God could be trying to protect you. He could be trying to protect you from more harm physically, mentally, emotionally, and even spiritually. It's okay to question God and ask Him why He took the person out of your life. You may not get the answer you want right away, but God will help you feel better day by day as you navigate your life without that person.

He will provide you with more true Godly friends so that your mourning and weeping will be turned to dancing. He will let you know that those people are sent from Him for your blessing. Once you start hanging out with your new Godly friends, you will be filled with a joy that can't be explained. So that's when you know that it's the joy that can only come from God Himself.

· ·

Whenever you go through difficulties with friends, say this
prayer: "Lord, please help me to find true friends that can only
come from you. Thank you for filling me with a joy that can't
be explained."

Frustration and Complaining

"Be joyful in hope, patient in affliction, faithful in prayer."
Romans 12:12

Have I prayed about things as much
as I've complained about them?

Have you ever found yourself complaining? Do your friends and family tell you to stop complaining? Maybe you complain about your homework, friendships, or even your home life. Maybe you complain about the rules and the curfew that your parents set up for you. When you complain, you are letting the Devil have control over your thoughts. Once he gets under your skin and into your mind, you can have a hard time resisting him. He will tell you that complaining isn't that big of a deal.

He will also tell you that letting your anger and frustration out on your family and friends feels good. For a short time, it might feel acceptable to you. But don't you feel worse after you've been complaining about too long? You feel more frustrated and mentally, emotionally, and even physically exhausted. Instead of complaining about your life, you can actually pray about it. Praying can bring you peace. It can take your focus off your problems to the One who can solve them. You can teach yourself to be joyful and full of hope and to be patient and faithful in prayer, in the midst of your circumstances.

• •

The next time you start complaining, you can say this prayer to yourself: "Lord, thank you for letting me know that prayer can change my life. Help me to pray instead of just complaining about my life."

Recognition

*"Whatever you do, work at it with all your heart,
as working for the Lord, not for human masters."*
Colossians 3:23

Am I doing things for God or
for recognition from others?

As a teenage girl, many things need your attention, from schoolwork to homework, chores, sports practice, and spending time with your family and friends. No matter what you have to do every day, whether it's chores or homework, make a list of your priorities. If you have schoolwork that needs to be done before you can hang out with your friends, make sure that your preferences are straight and that you do the schoolwork first. Even if you're having a hard time with a specific subject, just do your best. That is all anyone can ask of you. That's all God asks of you too. You can work on the task in front of you as if you're doing it for God.

You don't have to do things for worldly recognition. Nor do you have to do them, so your friends think that you're cool. If you keep your focus on God in every task you need to do, you'll go far in life. Doing your studies with a joyful heart and pleasing God is a much better plan than trying to please the world.

Whenever you want recognition for the things you do, you can say this prayer: "Lord, thank you for reminding me to do everything as if I'm doing it for you."

DEVOTION 47

Smart Money Habits

"His master replied, 'Well done, good and faithful servant!
You have been faithful with a few things; I will put you
in charge of many things. Come and share your master's
happiness!'
Mathew 25:21

Do I please God with my life?

All around you, there are temptations. There are temptations to not do your chores. If you don't do your tasks, you may not get any allowance. Your parents have taught you about the value of money and about putting your money into the bank. If you have a job, some of your paychecks should automatically go into the bank for savings for a rainy day.

If your parents see that you're careful with your money and don't spend it all in one place, they will know that you care about your future. If they see you being smart with your money, they will also give you other more significant responsibilities such as paying for your own car and insurance when you can drive. God also sees that you're smart with your money. He will reward you too. If He sees you being smart with the little things in your life, he will reward you with bigger, more important things.

Whenever you're tempted to not be smart with your money, you can say this prayer: "Lord, thank you that you and my parents are teaching me how to be smart with my money as a teen, so I can have more responsibilities as an adult."

Going to School Everyday

"May the God of hope fill you with all joy and peace as you trust in him, so that you may overflow with hope by the power of the Holy Spirit."
Romans 15:13

How can I fully put my trust in God?

Do you have hope in your life, or are you filled with dread about going to school every day? What makes you dread school? Your teachers, classmates, or the fear that you won't understand the material that's being taught? If you're struggling in school, there is nothing wrong with getting help. If you're falling behind, tell your teachers and parents. Explain to them how you're struggling; otherwise, they won't know that there's a problem.

If you tell your parents and teachers about your problem, they can get you the help you need, by bringing you a tutor or helping you through the tricky subject themselves. They can ask you questions about where you're struggling and figure out the best course of action for you to succeed in school. Once you start feeling more successful in school, your confidence will go up. Ask God to help you be brave enough to tell your parents or teachers the subject you're struggling with. Ask Him to fill you with His peace and joy as you trust in Him. He will help you understand schoolwork better.

• •

If you're struggling with school and are afraid to ask for help, you can say this prayer: "Lord, guide me in school and help me to understand the difficult subjects."

Being Helpful

"In everything I did, I showed you that by this kind of hard work we must help the weak, remembering the words the Lord Jesus himself said: 'It is more blessed to give than to receive.'"
Acts 20:35

When was the last time I helped someone?

People need help everywhere. Whether it's in your neighborhood, across town, or even across the world. Where have you seen the needs of others around you? Did you help someone cross the street safely? Did you comfort a friend or family member that was going through a hard time? Have you served meals to the homeless at your church or at a homeless shelter for a service project? How did it feel seeing others in need? Did it dawn on you just how blessed you really are with everything that you have? Didn't it make you feel good helping someone in your neighborhood or community that really needed it?

Whenever you see someone in need, reach out to them and see if you can help them in any way, whether it's big or small. No good deed is too short to do. It is more of a blessing to give to someone than it is to receive. It makes you feel good being able to help others and make their lives better. When you serve others, you're reflecting God's love.

• •

The next time you see someone in need, say this prayer: "Lord, please help me to see and attend to those in need. Help me be a reflection of you."

Serving without Expectations

*"Give, and it will be given to you. A good measure,
pressed down, shaken together and running over,
will be poured into your lap. For with the measure
you use, it will be measured to you."*

Luke 6:38

How can I give to people and not
ask for something in return?

Have you thought about the different ways you can help others in life? If you give to others while expecting something in return, you aren't giving to someone with God's love in your heart. As a teenager, it can be tempting to think, "what's in this for me? How does this benefit me?" It is more critical and even more special to give to those who cannot pay you back. Remember that helping people doesn't always have to reap a reward for you. If you give to someone out of the goodness of your heart, God will reward you.

If He sees you giving out of selfish desires, then He won't reward you. If you're not feeling like serving others willingly, then God tells you not to do it. He doesn't want you to operate with a sour heart. Don't give to others or help others unless you feel good about doing so. Whatever you give, you will also get. Any good measure will come back to you. Whatever you do, it will be done unto you.

. . . .

The next time you struggle with the thought of serving others,
you can say this prayer: "Lord, help me to want
to serve others willingly."

Malicious Gossip

"Do not let any unwholesome talk come out of your mouths, but only what is helpful for building others up according to their needs, that it may benefit those who listen."
Ephesians 4:29

Have I ever gossiped about anyone?

As a teenager, you hear gossip all the time, whether in school or on the cheerleading squad or on the sports team. If you have a job, you've probably heard gossip at the office too. As tempting as it can be to engage in the "small talk" of gossip, it's essential to realize just how damaging gossip can be. One phrase can be misunderstood. Then you can repeat something to someone else that may not be entirely true. One lie can ruin someone's reputation. You may just want to be in on the gossip that's in different groups, but if you hear someone talking wrong about someone else, you need to put a stop to it if you can. You wouldn't like anyone starting rumors about you, would you?

You don't have to engage in the gossip you hear. You can tell people that they are potentially hurting someone's reputation and that they could hurt a friendship beyond repair because of gossip. You can re-mind them that building people up is more important than hurting them. Look for ways to build others up instead of tearing them down. Build people up according to their needs.

The next time you hear someone gossip and hurt others, say this prayer: "Lord, please help me to build others up instead of hurting them."

DEVOTION 52

Forgiving Others

*"But if you do not forgive others their sins,
your Father will not forgive your sins."*
Mathew 6:15

Who do I need to forgive in my life?

Have you ever said, "I won't forgive you," to one of your friends after an argument? How did you feel after saying those words? Did you feel guilty, angry at yourself, or ashamed? It can take years to make a friendship and only seconds for the trust to be broken. Many times, after a massive fight with a friend, it can take many months or years to rebuild the relationship.

You need to know that God forgives you every day for each and every sin you've committed against Him, as long as you seek forgiveness full-heartedly. If God can forgive you for the sins you commit, how can you say that you won't forgive anyone else? If you don't forgive someone for their sins, then God will not forgive you for yours. Think about that for a minute. You want to be absolved from your sins, right? So, you should be quick to forgive others too.

. . . .

The next time you don't want to forgive someone, ask God to
change your heart and say this prayer: "Lord, please help me
to forgive others, no matter how they have hurt me. Thank you
for forgiving my sins."

Encouragement

"Therefore encourage one another and build each other up, just as in fact you are doing."
1 Thessalonians 5:11

How can I encourage someone today?

Have you ever needed encouragement after a hard day? What did you do to make yourself feel better? Did you take a hot bath or shower, read one of your favorite books, watch a favorite comedy, or snuggle your pet? Have you ever seen one of your friends struggling in school or in their personal life?

Here are some things that you can do to encourage your friend and lift their spirits. You can ask them if they'd like to get a snack at a restaurant, bring them their favorite drink from Starbucks or Dunkin Donuts, or bring them their favorite ice cream. You can also encourage them by letting them know that both you and God are with them through their challenging situation and that you're not going anywhere. Offer to pray for and with them. Offer to help them study for tests or help them with their homework whenever they need help. Tell them that they are strong enough and capable of getting through whatever hard time they are in. Just be present with them and ask them what they need, even if it's only a shoulder to cry on or someone to vent to.

- -

Whenever you see your friend needs encouragement, you can say this prayer out loud or in your heart: "Lord, please help me find ways to be an encouragement to my friend."

DEVOTION 54

Arguing with Parents

"Remind the people to be subject to rulers and authorities, to be obedient, to be ready to do whatever is good, to slander no one, to be peaceable and considerate, and always to be gentle toward everyone."

Titus 3:1-2

Am I gentle towards my parents?

Have you ever felt guilty after having an argument with your parents? Did you ever disrespect your parents? As a teenager, it can be hard to not yell at your parents when you want your way. You might think you deserve more freedom, while they might feel that you need to do better at handling your responsibilities you already have. Remember, you are still under your parents' roof, and you are still under their authority and rules. As much as they will drive you crazy, you also have to be careful not to speak ill of your parents no matter how annoyed you feel.

The Bible reminds you that you are subject to the authorities over your life and to be obedient. It also tells you to be ready to do whatever is right, which means being friendly to your parents, no matter how they make you feel. It is better to be peaceful with them and explain your feelings calmly than to raise your voice in anger at them. Ask God to help you remain gentle whenever you're having discussions with them.

• •

Whenever you want to yell at your parents, say this prayer instead: "Lord, please help me to be gentle in conversations I have with my parents."

Having Sex While I'm on My Period

"Do not approach a woman to have sexual relations during the uncleanness of her monthly period."
Leviticus 18:19

How will I react if my boyfriend wants to have sex with me outside of marriage while I'm on my period?

You will have your period every month from about age 13 on, and it can be quite embarrassing for some girls. It can cause you to bleed through your pants, cause intestinal issues for a few days, and cause severe cramps. What do you do if your boyfriend wants to have sex with you while you're on your period? You already know that you're not supposed to have sex with a man outside of marriage. It says in the Bible that no one should approach a woman to have sex with her while she is on her period.

It is messy, stinky, and very unsanitary—not to mention difficult and very uncomfortable for a girl—to have sex while she's on her period. You can explain that to your boyfriend. If he doesn't respect your boundaries, pray to God for wisdom about the situation, or just get out of that relationship altogether. A man should honor your expectations and boundaries.

• •

If you think about having sex while on your period, say this prayer: "Lord, please help me to remember that it's unclean to have sex while on my period. Help me to stand firm to my beliefs about what it says in your word. Thank you for your guidance in this new part of my life."

Temptation to Gossip

*"Keep your tongue from evil and
your lips from telling lies."*
Psalm 34:13

How can I keep my mouth from spreading lies
and keep my tongue from evil?

Have you heard the gossip that goes on in different groups in your school? Have you ever been tempted to engage in gossip with the other girls? The next time you hear one of the other girls say something mean about another kid, try not to engage with that conversation. Think about how you would feel if someone said something mean about you. Words can hurt. Once they're said, they can't be taken back. They can only be forgiven.

When someone gossips about another person, it can harm that person's reputation. Mean words can also hurt that person mentally and emotionally, and it can even harm them physically and spiritually. God warns you in the Bible to keep your tongue from evil and your lips from telling lies. That means always being aware of who you're hanging out with and being in tune with what you're hearing. It primarily means being in tune with what you're saying in front of others. If you're engaging in gossip about someone, stop. Remove yourself from the situation before you hurt someone with your words. Ask God to help you to guard your tongue and to think before you speak.

• •

The next time you're tempted to gossip, try saying this prayer:
"Lord, please help me to keep a guard over my mouth. Help me
to speak your truth and love with my words."

Being Discouraged

"Don't let anyone look down on you because you are young, but set an example for the believers in speech, in conduct, in love, in faith and in purity."
1 Timothy 4:12

How can I be a Godly example to others in my life?

Have you ever been discouraged because people aren't listening to you when you talk about Jesus? It can get discouraging telling others about Jesus only to have them scoff at you. Whatever you do, don't give up. It is essential to not let anyone look down on you just because you're a teenage girl who loves Jesus with all your heart.

Do not be ashamed of that or afraid to admit it to anyone you meet. Speak the love of God over your life, over your family and friends. It just might change their lives, and it will definitely change yours for the better. You can set an example for everyone in your life to always look to God, no matter what they might be going through. People will see Jesus through your actions, words, and reactions to the things they tell you.

Don't get discouraged because people think you're too young to talk about the goodness of God. You're never too young to tell others about Him. Share His love in every way possible and in every possible place, no matter how young you are.

Whenever you're discouraged about being His witness, say this prayer: "Lord, please help me to be an example of You in all I say and do."

DEVOTION 58

Forgive A Friend

"Then Peter came to Jesus and asked, "Lord, how many times shall I forgive my brother or sister who sins against me? Up to seven times?" Jesus answered, "I tell you, not seven times, but seventy-seven times." Mathew 18:21-22

How many times have I forgiven those who hurt me?

As a teenager, it's easy to have arguments with your friends. The arguments can be over makeup, grades, boys, school sports, and any topic in between. Have you ever told a friend in the middle of a heated argument, "I won't forgive you"? Has a friend ever said they won't forgive you for something you did? You need to ask yourself if losing a friend over not forgiving them is really worth it. Sometimes it takes you being the bigger person and forgiving your friend first to repair the relationship.

You also need to ask yourself, "How will I feel if I don't let this anger go?" Peter asked Jesus that same question. He asked, "how many times do I forgive my brother who sins against me, up to seven times?" Jesus says to forgive people who hurt you up to seventy-seven times. Forgiving a friend who hurt you will help give you the peace you long for. Ask God to help you to forgive the friends who have hurt you in any way.

• •

The next time you think about not forgiving a friend, you can say this prayer: "Lord, help me to want to forgive my friend, no matter how many times they hurt me."

Disobeying My Parents

*"Honor your father and your mother, so that you may live
long in the land the LORD your God is giving you."*
Exodus 20:12

How can I honor my mom and dad better?

Have you ever disobeyed your parents? Maybe you broke curfew, snuck out to see your friends when you should have been doing your homework, or snuck out while you were grounded. Think back to a time when you disobeyed them, and they found out about it. How did they punish you? Did you get grounded again with even stricter rules? Now think about how you reacted to them grounding you. Were you angry? Did you slam the door to your room?

The Bible says to honor your father and mother so you may live the long life that God is giving you. That means taking every interaction with your parents in stride and doing whatever they tell you to do, willingly, no matter how you may feel about it. It will make things easier for you and your parents if you can discuss things calmly, even if you disagree with the rules they have for you. As long as you live under their roof, you should listen to them. This not only honors them, but it also honors God. If you're having trouble honoring your parents, ask God to show you ways to honor them.

· ·

The next time you're tempted to disobey your parents, try
saying this prayer instead: "Lord, please help me find better
ways to honor my parents and you."

Carry the Burden

"Carry each other's burdens, and in this way, you will fulfill the law of Christ."
Galatians 6:2

How can I carry someone else's burdens today?

Have you ever felt like you had the weight of the world on your shoulders? Whenever you feel that way, what do you do to relieve your stress? Do you watch a movie or a comedy or take a hot bubble bath? Did you vent to a family member or friend? Venting may help you feel better now, but it doesn't really help you feel better in the long run. It is perfectly ok to cry to a friend or family member and tell them what is bothering you. They may help carry some of the load for you.

That is the great thing about being brothers and sisters in Christ. Everyone can count on each other. Whenever one person is struggling, their friend can carry their burden with them, so it's not so heavy. You can also carry someone else's burdens and help them feel better. God wants you to help others in any way that you can. Ask Him to give you ways to carry someone else's burdens. If you willingly carry someone else's burdens, you are fulfilling what Jesus asked of you. You know how good it feels to have burdens lifted off of you; just think of how good it must feel for someone else.

· ·

Whenever you see someone needs help, say this prayer:
"Lord, please help show me how to willingly carry
someone else's burdens."

Forgiving a Bully

*"You have heard that it was said, 'Love your neighbor
and hate your enemy. But I tell you, love your enemies
and pray for those who persecute you..."*
Mathew 5:43-44

How can I love my enemies and pray
for those who mistreat me?

Have you ever been bullied at school? No doubt, it's not an easy thing to get through, especially as a teenager. Have you ever told your family or friends you hate the person who's bullying you at school? You probably said that you hate them out of anger and frustration. Maybe you said that you hate them out of fear. There is a challenging verse to swallow in the Bible: love your enemies and pray for those who persecute (mistreat) you. You might be thinking, "Jeez, that's crazy! Why would I want to do that?! They hurt me. I want to want to hurt them back. Pray for my enemies?! That's really difficult!"

Instead of hating someone because of what they've done to you, try telling them how they've hurt you. Then simply say, "I'm praying that your day gets better." Most of the time, the person will be completely stunned into silence when you say you're praying for them. Ask God to help you pray for anyone who is bullying you. It will help heal your emotional wounds.

• •

The next time you're bullied, try saying this prayer:
"Lord, please help me to want to pray for the kids who bully
me. Help me to be kind to them."

Restraining Anger

"Let your conversation be always full of grace, seasoned with salt, so that you may know how to answer everyone."
Colossians 4:6

Do I answer with gentleness or with anger
in my conversations with my family?

Do you have a tendency to snap at people in the middle of conversations when things aren't going your way? How about having heated discussions with your siblings or parents? Every teenage girl has moments of anger, no matter what the topic of discussion is. No matter how you may feel, you can control your words, thoughts, and your actions. Taking control over yourself even when you feel angry takes a lot of self-discipline. It also takes a lot of patience with yourself.

Try your best to show restraint even if you're angry—answer people with the same respect that you'd expect them to give you. Even though you will mess up and show anger during certain conversations, God will give you the correct words at the right time. Every conversation, whether it goes well or not, is all a learning experience. God will help you know how to answer your parents and your siblings correctly. Ask Him for guidance in this area of your life. Do your best to be full of grace in every conversation.

The next time you want to shout in any conversation, try saying this prayer in your heart instead: "Lord, please help my conversations with anyone to be calm. Please teach me how to answer everyone kindly."

DEVOTION 63

Conflicted about Sex before Marriage

"Flee from sexual immorality. All other sins a person commits are outside the body, but whoever sins sexually, sins against their own body."
1 Corinthians 6:18

Have I ever committed a sin by having
sex before marriage?

"Come on! Sex isn't that bad!" "Having sex before marriage isn't a bad thing if you love the person!" "God won't punish you if you have sex outside of marriage." "Don't be such a good girl." "Don't tell everyone that sex before marriage is a sin because not everyone believes that." Those are all the whispers that you can hear as a teenager. Have you ever thought about whether you should believe your friends when they insist that premarital sex isn't a big deal?

If you've ever been conflicted about what you should know about premarital sex, look at this verse in the Bible. God warns you to flee from sexual immorality. He even further warns you that all other sins that you can commit are actually outside your body, but if you have sex before marriage, you're committing a sin on the inside of your body. That makes sex a very big deal. If you stay strong and don't have sex before you're married, you're not only honoring yourself and your body, you're also protecting your body. You're also honoring God when you stay pure until marriage.

• •

If you're conflicted about having sex before marriage, say this prayer: "Lord, please help me to honor you and my own body by staying pure until I'm married to the right person."

Staying Away from Alcohol

"Do not get drunk on wine, which leads to debauchery.
Instead, be filled with the Spirit..."
Ephesians 5:18

Have I been tempted to drink when I'm underage?

"Come on, have a sip." "One sip won't hurt you." "You don't know what you're missing." "You're no fun." Those are all things that you can hear when your friends find out you don't want to drink with them. You may be tempted to try a sip of alcohol just to see what it tastes like. Sometimes one sip is all it takes to want more of it. There are serious physical and even severe legal consequences for drinking underage. You could end up with a nasty hangover the next morning and feel sick to your stomach.

If you're at a party with your friends and you're able to drive, please don't drink and then drive. If you drink and drive, you will get caught by the cops and probably end up in the juvenile hall. Or you could get into a deadly accident and possibly hurt or kill yourself, your friends, or another innocent person. If you get into an accident, you could wreck the car you're driving. The next time you're tempted to drink underage, remember the consequences. God doesn't want you to get drunk. He wants you to be filled with His Holy Spirit.

• •

The next time you're tempted to drink, say this prayer: "Lord, please help me to never drink and drive. Help me to stay away from alcohol until I'm old enough to drink."

Excessively Proud and Boastful

*For everything in the world—the lust of the flesh,
the lust of the eyes, and the pride of life—comes
not from the Father but from the world."*
1 John 2:16

Am I giving in to my own desires—and the desires of this world—
or trying to please God?

Are you proud of yourself for the things you've accomplished in life? There is a difference between being proud and being too proud. You're allowed to be proud of your accomplishments, but continuously bragging about them and being prideful of your achievements is wrong. You can be proud of yourself while not bringing attention to yourself, saying, "Hey, look at me. Look what I've done." If you keep your head down and work hard as if working for the Lord in everything you do, you'll go far in life.

The Bible says everything in this world, including the pride of life, is not from God but from the world. The world and Satan say, "Hey, look at me, not at God! Why not brag about everything you have done? Everyone deserves to hear about the great things you've done." But God wants you to look towards Him for wisdom and guidance about life. He wants you to look towards Him, not towards your own pride. He wants you to be humble and to keep your energy focused on Him.

Whenever you're tempted to brag, say this prayer instead:
"Lord, please help me to be humble and to focus on you,
not on the ways of this world."

Resisting the Devil Within

"Submit yourselves, then, to God.
Resist the devil, and he will flee from you."
James 4:7

How can I submit to God and resist
the devil's attacks?

If you've ever struggled with feeling like the weight of the world is on your shoulders as a teenager, don't give up. Tell God how you're stressed out and tell Him exactly why you're struggling and what you're struggling with. If you're struggling with schoolwork, the death of a friend or a loved one, looking for work, or even struggling at the job you just got, the devil wants you to think you won't get through the hard times of your life. Resisting the devil takes self-discipline. It also means becoming aware of how he attacks your mind.

God wants you to come into His presence and enjoy every moment of your life. He wants you to submit yourself to His goodness and resist the devil by speaking positive thoughts over your life. You can say things such as, "I'm able to do anything with God at my side!" "You have no power over me, Satan. I'm God's child!" "Not today, Satan. I'm going to be joyful despite my circumstances." If you start resisting the devil as a teenager, he will flee from you throughout your life. Wouldn't you rather speak about the blessings in your life rather than the stressors?

. . . .

The next time the Devil attacks you, say this prayer:
"Lord, please help me to trust in you and to know
how to resist the Devil's attacks."

DEVOTION 67

Self-Control

"It teaches us to say "No" to ungodliness and worldly passions, and to live self-controlled, upright and godly lives in this present age..."
Titus 2:12

Do I have self-control?

What things do you say "no" to as a teenager? Do you say no to your parents, your siblings, or any other authority figures? Do you say no to your coaches when you feel they're pushing you too hard on the basketball court? Do you ever say no to your teachers when they ask you to read in class? Have you ever told your friends "no" when they try to convince you to drink, smoke, or do drugs with them?

The Bible says that you're supposed to say "no" to ungodliness and say "no" to worldly passions. This Bible verse also says to have self-control and to do your best to live a life that's pleasing to God. Saying "no" to having sex before marriage, drinking underage, smoking, or doing drugs requires discipline and self-control. Saying "no" to all of those things means you know the difference between right and wrong. If you develop a sense of right and wrong at a young age, it will help you know the difference between right and wrong later in your life too. If you say "no" to ungodly things as a teen and throughout your life, you're honoring God.

The next time you want to say yes to ungodly tendencies, say this prayer: "Lord, please help me to have self-control and say 'no' to ungodly tendencies."

My Focus in Life

*"Those who live according to the flesh have their minds
set on what the flesh desires; but those who
live in accordance with the Spirit have their minds
set on what the Spirit desires. The mind governed
by the flesh is death, but the mind governed by
the Spirit is life and peace."*
Romans 8:5-6

Do I set my mind on things of the flesh or on things of Heaven?

If you find yourself struggling with things as a teenager, you can easily ask yourself where your focus is in your life. If you're continuously stressed, letting the little things get to you, lashing out at the people around you, and are not enjoying the things you used to enjoy such as sports, hanging with friends, or listening to music, you may be trying to figure things out on your own. You may also be focusing too much on things of the flesh instead of things of Heaven that can bring you peace and joy.

The Bible says anyone that lives according to the flesh focuses on the desires of the flesh. However, anyone who lives with their minds set on things above have the peace of God. Have you taken the time to figure out where your focus is in life? You can have peace instead of frustration and stress.

The next time you need help refocusing in your life, say this prayer: "Lord, please help me to live with your peace in my life. Help me to stay focused on you every day."

Alcoholic Family Member

*"But now I am writing to you that you must not associate
with anyone who claims to be a brother
or sister but is sexually immoral or greedy,
an idolater or slanderer, a drunkard or swindler.
Do not even eat with such people."*
1 Corinthians 5:11

Is anyone in my family circle an alcoholic?

Do you have anyone that suffers from alcohol addiction in your family? How do you get through an angry outburst from them? Maybe your family tries to keep you away from what's really happening and keep you away from them when they're flying off the handle. You're a teenager, so if you have questions about anything that you've witnessed, it's completely ok to talk to someone you trust about that situation.

If the person that's the alcoholic is your own parent, talk to your other parent about the situation. Do not be afraid to lay all your questions in front of them. If you feel you need to speak to a pastor or another trusted adult such as a teacher or a coach, by all means, tell them how you're affected by the situation. God warns you to not even associate with someone who's a drunkard and even says to not eat with that person. You might think that statement is not what you'd expect from God. But He is trying to protect you from those people physically, emotionally, and even spiritually.

If you see a family member getting drunk, say this prayer:
"Lord, please help protect me from this person at all costs."

DEVOTION 70

Falling in Love

*"Daughters of Jerusalem, I charge you.
Do not arouse or awaken love until it so desires."*
Songs of Solomon 8:4

Have I met the person I'm going to marry?

You might be infatuated with someone in your teenage years. That's an entirely normal feeling as you explore new feelings of crushing on someone, loving someone, and being infatuated with someone. The critical thing to remember is that crushing on someone may not lead to other feelings of genuine love. Sometimes having a crush on a guy can lead to the guy liking you back, and then it can lead to you dating later on in life when you're both ready. Dating can eventually lead to marriage when the time is right.

Do you remember that you're not supposed to engage in sex until you're married? It says in the Bible to not arouse or awaken love until it's supposed to happen. You might end up finding the person you're going to marry by dating and figuring out how you and the other person connect. Ask God to help you have the wisdom and discernment about crushes, infatuation, and love. He will guide you as you go from single to a relationship, to engagement, and eventually—if it's His will—to marriage.

. . . .

The next time you think you're really in love with a guy, ask
God for guidance by saying this prayer: "Lord, please guide me
in my ways. Let me know what infatuation is, what is a crush,
and what is actually love that's
ordained by you."

77

Reliable Friends

"One who has unreliable friends soon comes to ruin, but there is a friend who sticks closer than a brother."
Proverbs 18:24

Do I have reliable friends that I can count on?

Think about your friends. Are they people you can turn to at any time, day or night? Or are they only there for you when it's convenient for them? It's important to make sure that you're in good company with your friends so that you can tell if one of them isn't good for you to be around. Teenagers change their minds a lot as to who they want to be friends with. One minute you can be in the "in" group, and the next minute, you can be cast out of the group.

The Bible says that anyone with unreliable friends soon comes to ruin. But the good news is that there is a friend who sticks closer than a brother. His name is Jesus. Jesus will always be there for you. He will never leave you guessing if He is for you or against you like some of your friends will. He will never abandon you when things get complicated. He will help you through all of your trials and give you the strength and courage to endure them. What more could you ask for in a friend? There is no friend like Jesus.

· ·

When you are struggling with real friendships, remember this prayer: "Lord, please help me figure out who my true friends are. Thank you that you're my truest friend."

Unbreakable Bond with Siblings

*"A friend loves at all times, and a brother
is born for a time of adversity."*
Proverbs 17:17

Do I feel a deep bond with my siblings?

Do you have siblings? If you do, you know how difficult it can be to get along with your sister or brother. You fight over makeup and clothes with your sister, and you fight over videogames with your brother. No matter how many times you fight with your siblings, you know that the bond you have is unbreakable.

If you don't have siblings, do you have friends who you consider family? Do you call them your brothers and sisters? It's essential to be trustworthy with your friends and let them know that they can always come to you for advice or chat when things are tough. A friend is someone who is there for you no matter what, through thick and thin. A brother or sister is also someone who you can turn to amid any hardships. If you have siblings who you consider your best friends, even if you drive each other crazy, then you're blessed. If you have friends who are considered family, you're blessed. You can be a friend that loves at all times and be a sister who helps your friends during their trials.

. . . .

Whenever you struggle to get along with your siblings or family friends, you can say this prayer: "Lord, please help me to be a true friend. Let my friends know they can count on me no matter what."

Working in Groups

"Two are better than one because they have a good return for their labor: If either of them falls down, one can help the other up. But pity anyone who falls and has no one to help them up."
Ecclesiastes 4:9-10

Do I like to do things in school on my own or in groups?

Do you like to do projects for school in groups, or do you prefer to do tasks independently? Sometimes it's easy for you to accomplish assignments for school your own. Even if someone offers to help you, you turn them down, saying, "I can do it myself." Other times, you have to work in groups and must divide the workload evenly amongst you and other kids in class.

When someone doesn't do their job within the group, everyone else has to do more work. But if everyone does their specific task to the best of their ability, the project will get done much more efficiently. God even says it's good for people to work in groups because working together is better than working alone. Plus, everyone gets a good grade on the assignment if you all work together. If anyone falls behind, you can help them finish their work too. You all can help each other complete the project successfully.

The next time you struggle with working in a group at school, try saying this prayer: "Lord, please help me to be willing to work with kids in school who need my help."

Being Kind to Others

"Do to others as you would have them do to you."
Luke 6:31

Have you been kind to people around you?

Gossip can hurt. It can destroy friendships. If you've ever heard someone you thought was a friend start nasty rumors about you, you know that kind of pain. You may feel as though your heart and trust with that person have been shattered into a million pieces and that you can never repair the relationship to what it once was. It is important to treat others as you would like to be treated and do to others as you would have them do unto you. That is the Golden Rule of the Bible.

If you don't want someone spreading gossip about you, then don't start spreading rumors or tell any gossip about them. If you're going to have friends, then be a friend. If you want to be included, then include others. If you're going to be accepted by others, then take others as they are. If you treat others the way they want to be treated and treat everyone with respect, they will treat you with the same respect. If you're kind to others, then people will be kind to you. If you want people to help you during hard times, willingly help others through their hard times. Ask God to help you treat others as you wish to be treated.

• •

If you struggle with being kind to others, say this prayer: "Lord, please teach me how to treat others the way I'd like to be treated."

Getting Closer to God

*"Come near to God and he will come near to you. Wash
your hands, you sinners, and purify
your hearts, you double-minded."*
James 4:8

How do I get closer to God?

You might be asking, "What things can I do to get closer to God every day? I want to get closer to Him and to share His goodness with people in my life, but I'm nervous." Here are some tips for you in your daily walk with God: You can read a daily devotional or a "verse-of-the-day" with an app on your phone, such as You Version. Reading a daily devotional gives you insight into yourself and how you're applying the devotional suggestions to your life. You can also start a weekly after-school Bible study with your friends. Hosting a Bible study can help you gain more lasting friendships.

You can figure out what topics to discuss and pick a new topic for each week. Holding yourself and the group accountable to do the weekly lessons helps the discussions go well. Every day, be mindful of the friends you have and think about who is benefitting from your walk with God. Walk away from the ones who aren't putting God as a priority. Keep your mind on things above, not on earthly things. Draw near to Him, and He will draw near to you.

If you're struggling to get closer to God, say this prayer: "Lord, please help me to want to know you more each day."

Sharing Joy and Sorrow

"Rejoice with those who rejoice;
mourn with those who mourn."
Romans 12:15

Have I rejoiced with my friends who were happy
and been there for the friends that are grieving?

Have you ever felt jealous that your friend got a really cool new make-up kit, that she was chosen for the cheerleading squad, or that she got an A on her Spanish test? It's easy to be jealous of your friend when she gets something that you really wanted. You might even start treating her differently because she brought something that you wanted. Have you ever acted that way towards your friend? It can be hard to learn to rejoice with a friend when she celebrates a victory in her life. But if you want someone to celebrate with you when you have a success, then you'll have to train yourself to rejoice for a friend when they're happy.

Similarly, if a friend is mourning, you have to train your mind to mourn with her and for her. If she is sad because she didn't get a good grade on the Spanish test, because she didn't make the cheerleading squad didn't get the new makeup kit, just be there for her. If you mourn with those who mourn and rejoice with those who rejoice, you're honoring God by being there for your friends.

• •

Whenever you struggle to rejoice or mourn with friends, say
this prayer: "Lord, please help me to rejoice and mourn with my
friends whenever each situation arises."

Jealousy toward Friends

"But if you harbor bitter envy and selfish ambition in your hearts, do not boast about it or deny the truth. Such "wisdom" does not come down from heaven but is earthly, unspiritual, demonic."

James 3:14-15

Am I envious of my friend's accomplishments?

If you struggle with bitterness, envy, and jealousy towards people who get where they want to be in life, you might want to reexamine your heart. Are you so blinded by jealousy, envy, and bitterness towards others that you can't even try to be happy for them? Take a few minutes and think about it. If you find that you're jealous of your friends, ask God to remove the jealousy from your heart.

If you're jealous that your friends get where they want to be in life, how do you expect anyone to rejoice for you when you get to where you want to be in life? Whether you're excelling in school, picking a great college, or being picked as the cheerleading captain, if you don't care when a friend is excelling in their life, why would they care when you're excelling in yours? God warns you not to boast about your selfishness and do not deny the truth: that this type of "wisdom" is earthly, unspiritual, and demonic. Ask God to soften your heart towards your friends. Ask Him to help you be happy when your friend is excelling.

Whenever you struggle with jealousy toward your friends, say this prayer: "Lord, please help me to not be jealous of my friend's accomplishments."

Strengthen My Faith

"He replied, "Because you have so little faith.
Truly I tell you, if you have faith as small as a
mustard seed, you can say to this mountain,
'Move from here to there,' and it will move.
Nothing will be impossible for you."
Mathew 17:20

In what areas do I need to strengthen my faith?

What big decisions do you have to make in your life? Are you deciding where to go to high school or what major to pursue in college? How about wanting to play numerous sports yet not being sure which one you should pick? Are you nervous to try out for the cheerleading squad and afraid that you won't be on varsity? Those are areas of life where your faith can be tested.

At times, it seems impossible to keep faith when you have important decisions to make. But Jesus offers you some reassurance. Even if you're unsure of what to do in any situation, He always gives you a way out of, around, and even through it. He tells you that if you have faith as small as a mustard seed and say to a mountain to jump, it will jump. How much more will even just a little faith help you in your life? You will make the right decisions with His help and guidance. Nothing will be impossible for you with Him at your side.

When you struggle with faith, remember this prayer:
"Lord, help strengthen my faith in you. Thank you that nothing is impossible for you."

Mobile Phone Addiction

*"No one can serve two masters. Either you will hate the
one and love the other, or you will be devoted to the one
and despise the other...."*
Mathew 6:24

Am I addicted to my phone?

Are you always on your phone? When you're out to dinner, are you not paying attention to the people you're with? How about when you're with your friends? Do you text someone when they're in the same room or sitting next to you? If you're always on your phone, you're missing out on so many great things in life. You're missing out on family talks and long overdue chats with your friends. You're also missing out on the beauty of the world around you if you're always on your phone. If you feel you can't go one hour without texting or checking a game's scores, then you actually do have an addiction.

You might say, "Addiction means I'm addicted to drugs or alcohol, not my phone." If you're always on your phone, even when people ask you to put it down, you're struggling with addiction. In the Bible, it says you can't have two masters. If you love your phone, you're probably struggling to make God a priority. God should be the Lord of your life, not your phone. Ask God to help take away your phone addiction.

The next time you're on your phone, say this prayer:
"Lord, please reveal how I can spend less time on my phone
and spend more time with the people around me."

Unconditional Love

*"Love is patient, love is kind. It does not envy,
it does not boast, it is not proud. It does not dishonor
others, it is not self-seeking, it is not easily angered,
it keeps no record of wrongs."*
1 Corinthians 13:4-8

Am I giving unconditional love to those around me?

Do you give unconditional love to everyone around you? How did Jesus love those that were unlovable? What does this teach you about loving people in your life? Jesus proved that love is not only a feeling that you can have, but that love is a choice you make every day. You may struggle to show unconditional love, but Jesus loved people with true unconditional love. He died for everyone's sins.

When you love, you're patient with people, even when you don't feel like being patient. You're kind to those who are unkind to you. You don't envy others. You aren't proud and boasting about the way things are going in life. When you love, you do your best not to dishonor people. Showing love towards others means not being easily angered and keep no record of wrongs. Even though you will fail at all of those things in your life, as long as you try to show unconditional love to everyone, even when you don't feel like it, then you're honoring God.

Whenever you struggle with giving unconditional love,
say this prayer: "Lord, please help me to show unconditional
love to everyone around me. Show me how to love even
when I don't want to."

Healing after Losing Grandparents

*"I consider that our present sufferings are not worth
comparing with the glory that will be revealed in us."*
Romans 8:18

Do I believe that I'll see my grandparents
again in Heaven?

Losing your grandparents is never easy, especially at a young age. What is the best memory you have with your grandparents? Maybe it was talking about Jesus while spending time together, or looking at photo albums and listening to the stories about their lives. Did you visit them in the hospital while they were sick? No matter how sick they may be, you can remind them that they have the hope of Heaven waiting for them. Once they are in Heaven, they won't suffer anymore, and their bodies will be made whole.

You can remember all the good times that you had with your grandparents and treasure them in your heart. You will miss them terribly. But you can also hold on to the hope that you will see them again one day when you get to Heaven. Let this verse bring you comfort: "your present sufferings can't even compare to the joy that is coming." Rejoice that you will see your grandma or grandpa when you get to Heaven. Rejoice in the fact that they are well. Rejoice that they are in paradise with Jesus, where they belong.

• •

Whenever you miss your grandparents, say this prayer:
"Lord, please help me to remember that I'll see my
grandparents again in Heaven."

A Pet Suffering

*"There is a time for everything and a season
for every activity under the heavens:
a time to be born and a time to die."*
Ecclesiastes 3:1-2

How can I help my pet?

Do you have a pet? Is it a dog or a cat? Are they your best friend? Do you spend every minute with them when you come home from school? Do you play fetch and take them for walks? When your pet gets older, he or she may slow down and not be able to walk or eat as well as they used to. It will be difficult to see them deteriorate before your eyes.

No one wants their pet's health to deteriorate, but unfortunately, that will happen. The Bible says that "there is a time for everything, a time for every activity under heaven: a time to be born and a time to die." Even though you don't want your pet to die, they will. They will stick around and hang on for you, but you have to decide if you want them to suffer more than they already are. It might be better to let them be released from their suffering and to let them go in peace, surrounded by your love. Even though you won't want to say goodbye, it could be the best thing to do.

. . . .

If you see your pet suffering, say this prayer: "Lord, please guide me in the decisions I make for my pet's health."

Dealing with Serious Illness

*"My flesh and my heart may fail, but God is the
strength of my heart and my portion forever."*
Psalm 73:26

Do I believe God will help me through my illness?

If you're dealing with a severe illness such as cancer or diabetes, it can be easy to get discouraged about your health. Lots of teenagers your age go through the same thing. In the beginning, there's often the shock and denial that this is happening to you. There are doctor's appointments and treatments that you go through to stay healthy. You're often left wondering if you will beat cancer and get the right treatment.

Even if you struggle with the fear that you will not beat the illness you have, there's hope through Jesus Christ that you can hold on to in your times of pain, treatment, and discouragement. Even though your heart and flesh may fail, you can rest in the strength of God. You can rest assured physically, emotionally, and mentally that God is with you through every minute, second, and day of your life. Let His words encourage and strengthen you for the days ahead. Do not give up because God is walking with you through everything you have to go through. God will give you the strength that you didn't know you had within you.

If you're going through an illness, say this prayer:
"Lord, thank you for being my strength during my
illness diagnosis and treatment."

Being Forgiven for Sins

*"As far as the east is from the west,
so far has he removed our transgressions from us."
Psalm 103:12*

Do I believe that I'm genuinely forgiven by God?

Have you committed a sin that you didn't think God would forgive you for? As a teenager, you can often believe that God will not forgive you for your sins. Or if you keep doing the same thing over and over, even though you're trying not to, you may not know how you will even approach God to ask Him for His forgiveness. If you're struggling with finding the true forgiveness from your sins that God is willing to give you, talk to someone you trust about it.

It can be a friend, parent, pastor, counselor, or an extended family member. Tell them about your sins and your struggle to overcome them. You can be honest and tell them that you don't think God will forgive you for the things you've done. The good news is that God promises you that if you ask for forgiveness, your sins are forgiven fully with no condemnation from God. You can stop blaming yourself for messing up because God already knew that you would mess up and sin. Yet, He doesn't—and won't ever—hold it against you.

• •

The next time you struggle to believe that you're forgiven, say this prayer: "Lord, help me to believe your promise that all of my sins are forgiven fully."

Praying for Patience

"But if we hope for what we do not yet have,
we wait for it patiently."
Romans 8:25

Do I have the hope of Jesus in my heart?

As a teenager, you want confirmation of things right now, whether through a phone call, instant message, or a text. You might wish to plans with friends to be confirmed immediately. While some girls want things to be planned out in detail, some teenage girls don't mind doing things spontaneously. You often wait impatiently for your friends to call or text you back. You get excited about hanging out with your friends every chance you get. Did you know that you can have that same excitement about waiting for Heaven? You get so used to waiting impatiently, you might be asking, "How do I wait patiently for the things that I don't have? How do I wait patiently for God and wait patiently for Heaven?"

You can wait patiently for Heaven by declaring the good news of Jesus over your life. If you train yourself to wait patiently for the things you don't have, you will be much more appreciative when you receive them. As a Christian, you have the hope of Jesus in your heart, even if you can't yet see Him in person. You will see Him when you get to Heaven.

• •

If you're struggling with waiting patiently, say this prayer:
"Lord, please help me hold on to your hope in my life."

God Reads My Mind

*"For where two or three gather in my name,
there am I with them."*
Mathew 18:20

Do I believe God hears me when I pray with a friend?

Sometimes it can seem that God isn't even listening to you when you pray. You may have burning questions about your life and the way your life is going. Sometimes you may not be sure of how to approach God about how things are going in life. Do you want to pray with your friends about your future? Even if you pray alone, rest assured God hears you. But it's even better for you if you pray with one or two other people, whether it's with family members or your friends. God tells you that where two or three gather in His name, He is with them.

Even when you think He may not be listening to you, He knows what is on your mind before you even utter a word. Praying with other people helps you see things differently. Praying with other people also helps you know that you aren't the only person going through a difficult situation. It will open your eyes to how to pray for your and other people's needs. Let it bring you comfort to know that God is right there with you when you're praying with others.

Whenever you're struggling to figure out what to pray for, say this prayer: "Lord, thank you for knowing what's on my mind and that I can come to you by myself or with a friend."

Praying for Terminally Sick Friends

*"Jesus answered him, "Truly I tell you,
today you will be with me in paradise."*
Luke 23:43

Do I believe that my friend will be with God in Heaven?

Watching your friend go through cancer can be very difficult. You may not know how to react when they tell you how they're feeling. Just be there for them if they're sick, hurting, or fighting depression. Be the light of Jesus to them in the middle of their darkest times. If you're able to face time with them through their treatments to let them know that you're with them through it. If they're depressed because of fighting cancer, you can share your favorite Bible verses with them, make them laugh with funny jokes, and cook meals for them. It's never easy to see your friend fighting an incurable disease.

If they are told that they don't have long to live, just make the most out of every day that you have left with them. Visit them and call them as often as you can. If they come to you with doubts about salvation, you can tell them what Jesus said as He was on the cross: "Truly I tell you, today you will be with me in paradise." You can reassure them that if they know Jesus as their Savior, not only will you see each other again in Heaven, but Jesus will welcome them home with open arms.

• •

If a friend is sick, say this prayer: "Lord, please welcome my
friend to Heaven when their time comes."

Stand Up Against Bullying

*"Though one may be overpowered,
two can defend themselves. A cord of
three strands is not quickly broken."*
Ecclesiastes 4:12

Have I defended a friend that was bullied in school?

Have you had a friend go through a hard time with bullies at school? What did you do to help them through it? Did you tell the bullies to leave your friend alone? Did you tell one of the teachers or coaches and ask them to intervene for your friend? Even if you and your friend are afraid to stand up to the bullies, you can still help your friend. You can remind them that you'll always be in their corner if they need help. Just as God is always with them when they are being bullied.

You can also remind them of what God says; even though they might be overpowered when dealing with the bullies, two can defend themselves. If you, your friend, and God are all together, then God can stop the bullies from hurting your friend. There is nothing that God won't help your friend through. God wants you to come to your friend's defense. He wants your friend to stick up for themselves.

• •

The next time you see a friend being bullied in any way, say this prayer: "Lord, please help me stand up for my friend that's being bullied. Please protect them."

Holding a Grudge Against Friends

'Do not seek revenge or bear a grudge against anyone among your people, but love your neighbor as yourself. I am the Lord."
Leviticus 19:18

Have I have ever wanted revenge against a friend?

Grudges among teenage girls are all too common occurrences. Did a friend start a rumor about you, say mean things to your face, or cause other friends to turn their backs on you? Are you being humiliated by a friend? You may have thought, "I want them to feel the same way I feel right now. I'm hurt, and they deserve to feel the same way that I feel!"

Even though it's tempting to treat that person the same way they treated you, the Bible warns you not to seek revenge against a friend. God warns you not to bear a grudge among your friends. Instead of hurting that person back, God wants you to love your friend as you love yourself. Even though it may feel good to say something mean to them, it is better to be calm. He also wants you to try to make amends with the person by calmly explaining how they made you feel. Ask God to remind you of the good times you had with your friend instead of throwing the friendship away. He will guide your words.

Whenever a friend hurts you, try saying this prayer: "Lord, please guide my words if a friend has hurt me. Help me to talk to them nicely and explain how I feel."

Being Mocked for Following Jesus

"Blessed are you when people insult you, persecute you and falsely say all kinds of evil against you because of me. Rejoice and be glad, because great is your reward in heaven...."

Mathew 5:11

Have I been made fun of because of my passion for Jesus?

Have you often been made fun of because you always talk about Jesus? Do you get called a "Jesus freak"? Even though getting made fun of can hurt, there is nothing wrong with telling the people around you about God. If you're passionate about Jesus and what He has done for you, there is absolutely no reason to stop declaring His praises for the things He has done in your life. It even says in the Bible that you are blessed when people insult you and falsely say mean things about you when you're talking about Jesus.

You don't have to let their words get to you. You can be proud that you're passionate about Jesus. You can also rejoice and be glad because God will reward you when you get to heaven for telling others about Him. Don't give up your passion for Him or stop talking about Him because you are making a difference for His kingdom, no matter what people say about you. You know deep in your heart that you're doing the right thing.

. . . .

If you are made fun of for following Jesus, you can say this prayer in your heart or out loud: "Lord, please help me to keep declaring your good news through my life."

Judging Others

*"You, therefore, have no excuse, you who pass judgment
on someone else, for at whatever point you judge
another, you are condemning yourself, because you who
pass judgment do the same things."*
Romans 2:1

Where do I need to stop passing judgment in my life?

Judging others can be a hard habit to break, especially as a teenager. You may judge other kids at school for how they walk, dress, look, or how they talk. You may judge them because they were adopted or because they have family problems. If they read too much, you may call them a nerd. You may have even been judged for different reasons in your life, such as struggling with certain subjects in school, being famous, or reading too much.

You may have even been judged for following Jesus and telling others about Him. If you don't like it when others judge you, do your best to remember not to judge anyone else. It warns in the Bible to not pass judgment on anyone. Whenever you judge someone, that same judgment will be used against you. Whenever you judge someone, you're condemning yourself. Ask God to remind you not to judge someone and to fill your heart with kindness.

· ·

When you start judging someone, try saying this prayer:
"Lord, please show me areas where I need to stop
judging people in my life."

98

Saying Things You Later Regret

"If it is possible, as far as it depends on you,
live at peace with everyone. Do not take revenge,
my dear friends, but leave room for God's wrath,
for it is written: "It is mine to avenge; I will repay,"
says the Lord."
Romans 12:18-19

Who in my life do I need to live at peace with?

You might think that it's impossible to live in peace with everyone in your life. Living in harmony with your parents, siblings, friends can be complicated. Sometimes, you just snap and say things you later regret. You're often left thinking, "Why did I say that in that way? I didn't really mean it. I really hurt their feelings. I didn't mean to! Lord, show me how I can live in peace with people in my life."

The good news is, God gives you ways to live at peace with everyone in your life. He even says, "if it is possible," because you won't be able to live at peace with everyone. He wants you to be nice to everyone and let the little things go. If there is something that needs to be discussed, try calmly explaining how you feel. Don't seek revenge against anyone who wronged you because everyone that hurt you will be avenged by the Lord. Do your best to live in peace and harmony with everyone, even when it's complicated.

Whenever you start to lose your cool, say this prayer:
"Lord, please remind me to live in peace with everyone."

Being Nice to Enemies

"If your enemy is hungry, feed him; if he is thirsty, give him something to drink. In doing this, you will heap burning coals on his head." Do not be overcome by evil, but overcome evil with good."
Romans 12:20-21

How can I help enemies in my life?

Have you ever seen people that hurt you, struggling in school, or struggling to make friends? Even though it can be tempting to turn away from them because of what they've done to you, Jesus talks about being nice to your enemies. If you see them thirsty, give them a drink. If they're hungry, share some of your lunch with them. You might be thinking, "That's crazy; why should I be nice to someone who has hurt me?"

Jesus says being nice to people who hurt you is like placing burning coals on their heads. That means that when you're nice to them, it can completely shock them. Think about it this way, doesn't it feel better to do something nice for someone, no matter what they did to you? Doesn't it feel good to help someone? Jesus also warns you to not be overcome with evil but to overcome evil thoughts and deeds by doing good to those who hurt you. Ask God how you can be nice to people that hurt you.

• •

Whenever someone hurts you, say this prayer: "Lord, please teach me to help those who hurt me when I see their need."

Honor and Love

*"Be devoted to one another in love.
Honor one another above yourselves."*
Romans 12:10

How can I honor people in my life?

In what ways can you honor the people in your life? Have you ever showed devotion to someone in your life, whether your boyfriend, sibling, parents, or grandparent? There are many ways you can honor the different people in your life and be devoted to them in love.

You can honor your parents by cleaning your room, the bathroom, and cleaning the house. You can honor your parents by doing laundry, so they don't have to do it. You can also make them dinner without being asked.

You can honor your boyfriend by helping him in any way that he needs it. If he struggles in school, encourage him and help him figure out his homework or study for his test. If he struggles with people in his family, just be there for him and offer to pray with him as he navigates that part of his life.

You can honor your siblings by helping them through homework they may be struggling with within school.

You can honor your grandparents by getting food and running errands for them and by cleaning their house without being asked.

• •

Whenever you want to honor someone but aren't sure how, you can say this prayer: "Lord, please help me to love and honor the people in my life every way I can.".

Dealing with Temperamental People

"Do not make friends with a hot-tempered person, do not associate with one easily angered, or you may learn their ways and get yourself ensnared."
Proverbs 22:24-25

Do I know someone who gets angry quickly?

Do you have a friend or a family member that gets angry at the drop of a dime? How do you react to their anger? Do you shy away or calmly tell them to relax? You may not know what to do when you're around an angry person. You don't want to say or do something that would cause them to explode. It can feel like you're walking on eggshells all the time. You might even be anxious whenever you're around them. That's a routine flight or fight response.

The Bible warns you not to make friends with an angry person and not associate with them because you might pick up their bad habits of blowing up over nothing. You don't want to be in the same mindset as an angry person. Distance yourself from them every chance you get. The less time you're around them, the better off you will be. Though you might have to cut them out of your life, it is a better idea than letting them wreak havoc on your life. Ask God for guidance and His strength in this situation.

Whenever you're around an angry person, say this prayer:
"Lord, please help me to stay calm, but to also know when to walk away from this person."

Whenever You Get Rebuked

*"If anyone will not welcome you or listen
to your words, leave that home or town
and shake the dust off your feet. "*
Mathew 10:14

Have I experienced someone rebuking
my faith in Jesus?

If you're trying to spread the good news of Jesus with everyone in your life, and they keep rejecting the things you're saying, you can walk away. Jesus says if anyone does not listen to what you're saying about Him, you can leave that home or town. You might be thinking, "Well, if I try telling people about Jesus, I can't just walk away from them, can I?" The "anyone" in this verse means people who won't listen to you, including family. You can walk away from them if they don't accept Jesus.

The "anyone" also means your friends. If they don't accept the things you tell them about Jesus, then you have every right to walk away from them because they may not ever listen to you.

Remember, it's your choice to tell your friends and family members about Jesus, but it's their choice whether they accept Him in their lives and in their hearts or not. That's the free will God gives everyone. Even if they don't get Him, you know you did the right thing. Don't feel guilty about walking away from them.

· ·

If you struggle to walk away from someone who hasn't accepted
God in their life, say this prayer: "Lord, please help me to not
feel guilty for walking away from people who won't accept you."

God Intercedes on My behalf

"In the same way, the Spirit helps us in our weakness. We do not know what we ought to pray for, but the Spirit himself intercedes for us through wordless groans."
Romans 8:26

Do I believe God intercedes for me?

It can be very tough to know what to pray for as a teenager. Sometimes you literally may not know how to pray your thoughts out loud. It's okay to not know what to pray for in your life. There is even a verse in the Bible that when you don't know what to pray for, the Holy Spirit intercedes for you with groans that you can't understand. This means that even when you can't figure out what's in your heart or on your mind, and you can't figure out ways to put your feelings into words, Jesus knows exactly how you're feeling, no matter what you are going through.

Whether it's a breakup with a boyfriend, an unexpected falling out with a friend, an argument with a sibling, a discussion with your parents, or just struggling to fit in at school, Jesus knows exactly how you're feeling. He also knows what you need at precisely the right time. So even when you don't know what to say, you can take comfort knowing that the Holy Spirit is interceding to God for you on your behalf.

If you can't figure out what to pray for, say this prayer: "Lord, thank you that you're always interceding on my behalf, no matter what I may be going through."

104

DEVOTION 98

Whenever You Sin

*"For all have sinned and fall short of the glory of God,
and all are justified freely by his grace through the
redemption that came by Christ Jesus."*
Romans 3:23-24

Even though I sin, do I believe I receive
redemption from God?

Even though you will have struggles, lose your temper, and even be confused about which paths to take in your life as a teenager, you can take comfort in God's promises in the Bible. Even though you sin, you are learning from your mistakes every day. You are learning how to be a better person and a better Christian through each of those experiences.

The next time you are tough on yourself because of a mistake you've made, or if you're tempted to judge a friend or a family member because of a mistake they made, remember that God freely forgives you for every mistake you've ever made. You are justified by grace through faith and by the redemption that God gives you through your salvation in Jesus. No matter what you're going through as a teenager, God is walking with you through every experience. He will guide you in every decision. Whether it's in school, on the sports team, or deciding what you want to do with your life, God is always with you. Seek God in all you do, and He will guide you.

Whenever you struggle with sin, say this prayer: "Lord, please
help me to never give up during my struggles. Thank you for
giving me forgiveness and salvation."

Grandma / Grandpa

*"He heals the brokenhearted
and binds up their wounds."
Psalm 147:3*

Do I feel that God can heal my grandma/grandpa?

Have you prayed for a miracle for your grandma's health to be restored? Is she sick with cancer or another illness? You hate seeing your grandma or grandpa losing strength and being sick. Just be there for her in the midst of her suffering, to hold her hand and tell her that everything will be ok. Tell her that everything will work out. Give her the hope that can only be found in Jesus. Share the good news of Jesus with her and pray for her and with her. There is nothing wrong with having the faith that God can heal your grandma because there are times where He will heal people from their sickness and their wounds.

If it is God's will for your grandma/grandpa to be healed, He will allow it to happen in His timing and in His way. Sometimes you have to just let God do what He knows is best for your grandma/grandpa. Even if your grandma/grandpa doesn't get healed on Earth, He will heal her when she gets to heaven. Whenever your grandma goes to Heaven, God will be with you through that pain. He will stay close to you as you navigate life without her on Earth.

· ·

Whenever you see your grandma/grandpa struggling, say this
prayer: "Lord, please heal my grandma if it's your will."

God's Will for My Life

*"Why, you do not even know what will happen tomorrow.
What is your life? You are a mist that appears for a little
while and then vanishes.
Instead, you ought to say, "If it is the Lord's will,
we will live and do this or that."*
James 4:14-15

Am I living according to God's will?

What do you waste your time worrying about as a teen? Your grades, school, what college you might attend, what job you will get in the future? What with worrying about your family's future or how your relationship with your boyfriend will work out? Why worry about what would happen in the future when you don't even know what will happen in your day-to-day life? The Bible says that your life is a mist that appears for only a little while and then vanishes.

Instead of worrying about what will happen in your life, you can change your attitude and enjoy things even more. Instead of giving in to worry or dread, you can say, "If this is God's will, I will do it. If it isn't God's will, then I won't do it." Ask God and pray for discernment about what His will is in your life, and you will get direct answers from Him.

· ·

Whenever you struggle to figure out God's will for your life, you
can say this prayer: "Lord, thank you for giving me discernment
about what your will is for my life. Guide me to know what
paths to take."

Made in the USA
Coppell, TX
28 September 2021